The Leslie Grantham Story

Myra Hindley – Inside the Mind of a Murderess

The
Leslie Grantham Story

The Secret Life of 'Dirty Den'

JEAN RITCHIE

ANGUS
& ROBERTSON
PUBLISHERS

ANGUS & ROBERTSON

16 Golden Square, London W1R 4BN,
United Kingdom, and
Unit 4, Eden Park, 31 Waterloo Road,
North Ryde, NSW, Australia 2113.

First published in the United Kingdom by
Angus & Robertson (UK) in 1989

Typeset by the Word Shop, Rossendale, Lancashire

Printed in Great Britain by Richard Clay Ltd, Bungay, Suffolk

British Library Cataloguing in Publication Data

Ritchie, Jean
  The Leslie Grantham story: inside the mind of 'Dirty Den'
  1. Television drama series in English. EastEnders.
  Acting. Grantham, Leslie
  I. Title
  791.45'028'0924

ISBN 0 207 16241 7

Contents

AUTHOR'S ACKNOWLEDGEMENTS

With thanks to: Ian Hepburn, Alan Lamprell, Kevin O'Sullivan,
James Wright and, most of all, Martin Smith.

Foreword

Leslie Grantham is the most exciting popular actor to emerge in Britain for years. It was his seedy charm as Dirty Den that captivated millions of viewers, and put the BBC's soap 'EastEnders' at the top of the audience polls. He combines the Cockney cheek of Michael Caine, the rough-edged power of Bob Hoskins and the menacing sex appeal of Robert de Niro. Yet his real-life story is more astounding than any part he has played on stage or screen. As a young man he committed murder, and has served eleven years in prison. He is secretive and defensive about his past and his personal life. To find the man behind the mask, I have had to probe into the parts of his life he would prefer to keep hidden.

This is the inside story of the real Leslie Grantham.

Jean Ritchie

CHAPTER 1

Childhood

Leslie Michael Grantham was born on 30 April 1947, in a two-bedroom basement flat at 12 Flodden Road, Camberwell, London SE5. The war had been over for two years, but Britain was still firmly in the grip of post-war austerity. Food was rationed. Clothing was officially off ration, but shortages in the shops and lack of money provided their own stringent restrictions.

The Budget two weeks before he was born had caused universal dismay by putting 1s (5p) on a packet of twenty cigarettes – in the days when a packet cost only the equivalent of 24p. Both Leslie's parents smoked, so it was an added strain on their family budget. There were dock strikes in London and Glasgow, holding up precious imports, and there was a miners' strike in Durham which was exacerbating the already chronic shortage of fuel.

Leslie was a healthy eight-and-a-half-pound baby, born at home between six o'clock and seven o'clock in the evening, with two Red Cross-trained neighbours helping his mother, Adelaide, with the birth. It was her second baby – her first son, John Walter, had been born two years and three months earlier. Baby clothes had been carefully stored away and were brought out for Leslie.

Five hours after Leslie was born, something happened that would make the headlines in all the newspapers the following morning: a taxi driver was shot and killed for money. George Tyler, a thirty-six-

year-old cabbie from Birmingham, picked up a fare at
the station there, a man in RAF uniform who wanted to
travel to Derby. Thirty miles from Birmingham, just
outside Burton, Tyler was shot three times and robbed.
It was a big front page news story in all the popular
papers, and if Leslie's mother was feeling fit enough to
glance at a paper the morning after her second son's
birth, she almost certainly read it. . . .

Adelaide Victoria Grantham was twenty-five when
her son Leslie was born. She had been married for
three years to Walter William Grantham, known as
Wally, seven years older than her and a clerk working
for Boots the Chemist. They met when Adelaide came
to London to work in the parcels office of the London
North East Railway during the war. In 1942 Wally,
then a colour sergeant with the Royal Fusiliers, lost his
hand and the lower part of his right arm when a
grenade he was holding exploded. It happened at an
army training base, where he was demonstrating the
use of grenades to recruits. The pin had not been removed, but the grenade was faulty. Wally was lucky to
escape without more severe injuries: the soldier in front
of him and the one behind him were both killed by the
force of the blast. He had served with the regiment in
Belgium and France and had been one of the thousands
evacuated from Dunkirk in 1940. His injury meant the
end of his war service – perhaps a heavily disguised
piece of luck, because in 1944 his regiment suffered
heavy losses at the Battle of Monte Cassino in Italy,
where many of Wally's friends and comrades died.

Before the war he had worked as a printer, but
without his hand he could not go back into that trade.
So, after convalescence and the fitting of an artificial
arm and hand, covered with a leather glove, Wally was
taken on as a clerk by Timothy Whites, a large retail
chemist that later amalgamated with Boots. Within
three years he rose to become assistant transport man-

ager for his branch and then transport manager. He was to work for Boots for thirty-nine years.

Wally is a Londoner born and bred: his father, another Walter, was a leather worker born in Bermondsey but living in Camberwell when Wally was born on 12 December 1915 – the same day as Frank Sinatra. His mother, Leslie's grandmother, was Beatrice May Grantham, an independent woman who became a Labour councillor for Southwark before the Second World War, when it was rare for women, especially working-class women, to have the drive to go into local politics. She was also a captain in the Salvation Army.

Leslie's mother, Anne, is not a Londoner. Her father was a commercial traveller and her mother a nurse. At the time of Anne's birth they were living in Gloucestershire, but her mother originally came from Ware in Hertfordshire, and eventually settled back there. Leslie's maternal grandmother died there in October 1988, but her two sisters, his great-aunts are still living there. Although his mother was christened Adelaide she never liked it, and early in life adopted the name of Angela, which her husband Wally later shortened to Anne.

Anne's maiden name was Flinders, which naturally gave rise to the nickname Polly. She has a distinguished family tree: Leslie Grantham's ancestors on his mother's side had a tradition of adventuring and exploration. Captain Matthew Flinders, who lived in the eighteenth and early nineteenth century, was one of the earliest explorers of the coast of Australia. He mapped it for British shipping and wrote a very valuable scientific book about his work. He was the first to discover and correct the compass errors caused by iron in ships, and the vertical bars of soft iron placed in front of or behind a ship's compass to this day to compensate for these disturbing magnetic effects are known as Flinders

11

Bars. There are also some mountains in Australia known as the Flinders Range.

Matthew Flinders' younger cousin was one of his crew on the voyages of exploration round Australia, and later went on to become an even more famous explorer. Sir John Franklin was one of the earliest explorers of the Arctic; he traced twelve hundred hitherto unknown miles of the North American coast; and he was lieutenant general of Van Diemen's Land, now called Tasmania, in the period when convicts from Britain and her empire were being shipped there in great numbers. He died on another polar expedition, while searching for the North West Passage – which he was the first to discover, although he did not live to enjoy the celebrity it brought him. A monument in Westminster Abbey commemorates his work and the devotion of his wife, who raised the money for an expedition to find out what had happened to her husband and the 128 men who had travelled with him.

Despite these illustrious forebears, life for young Leslie and his brother John was tough. They were part of the 'bulge', the population explosion that occurred in the immediate post-war years. It was not an easy time for any parents: a week after Leslie was born a ban on the use of gas or electricity to heat homes was due to come into force for the summer months, until the end of September. But as May 1947 was the coldest May for six years, Emanuel Shinwell, the Minister of Fuel and Power, allowed heaters to be used for an extra week.

After the birth of Leslie, the basement flat in Flodden Road was becoming crowded. When Adelaide became pregnant with her third child, the family were rehoused in a council house on a new estate in St Pauls Cray, Orpington, Kent, run in those days by the London County Council. It was one of many new housing estates springing up to accommodate the country's burgeoning number of young families. It was in the new house in Clarendon Way, shortly after the family arrived, that Leslie's sister Angela was born. Two years later, again just before the birth of a baby, the family exchanged houses for one in Ringshall Road, also in St Pauls Cray.

The fourth and youngest of the Granthams was another boy, Philip, born on his mother's thirtieth birthday. A fifth baby, a girl, was born several years later, but lived only for a month before she died of kidney failure. Leslie's mother was thirty-nine at the time, and it took her a long time to recover physically from the birth and emotionally from the death of her baby. It was at that time, while she was quite ill, that all the children learned to take care of themselves. Leslie had to share the cooking with the others, although it was Angela who bore the brunt of the rest of the housework.

When they were living in St Pauls Cray the children went to Leesons Hill Junior and infants' school, a new school built for the housing estate. John, Leslie's older brother, was the first head boy there. But when Leslie was ten years old, the family moved again: another council house exchange, this time for a three-bedroomed house on Tillingbourne Green, St Mary Cray.

The estate took its name from a large expanse of green around which the housing estate had been imaginatively developed. The green was irregular and hilly: an ideal play arena for the children of the estate, and the main attraction for the Grantham family in moving there. The house had a small front garden and a patch of ground at the back. John and Leslie shared a bedroom, and Philip and Angela shared until Leslie left home at sixteen, when Angela got a room of her own.

After the move to St Mary Cray Leslie, Angela and Philip transferred to Poverest Road junior school. Older brother John had already passed his eleven-plus examination, and was offered a choice of places at grammar school or technical school. Because he preferred maths to English, Wally and Anne decided to send him to Dartford Technical School, an all-boys school. Here John went from being top of the class at junior school, a big fish in a small pond, to being one of many equally bright boys, just scraping by. He hated it, and towards the end of his second year he was so unhappy that he ran away.

It was a traumatic event for the whole Grantham family, for John was missing from home for seven weeks. The police were alerted, and Wally and Anne were distraught. Although they tried to treat their children equally, John was always the favourite.

During this time he lived rough in the woods, using a tent loaned to him by another kid and eating food smuggled to him by his friends at the local secondary modern school. They would save him part of their school lunches: he'd get a slice of bread with ham on one side and cold rice pudding on the other. On one occasion a policewoman saw him and asked why he wasn't in school. John told her he had an appointment at the Cray Valley Hospital. It was only when he had disappeared that she realized Cray Valley was a maternity hospital, and she had to call on Anne Grantham and shame-facedly report that she had probably seen her son but had not apprehended him.

When John finally came home a family conference was called, and eventually the local education authority agreed that he should transfer from Dartford Technichal School, the root of his unhappiness, to the local secondary modern, Herne's Rise. That meant that big brother John started at Herne's Rise at the same time as Leslie, who did not pass his eleven-plus. John arrived with a tough reputation: a Dartford Technical drop-out, and a local hero to the other kids for living rough in the woods. The staff were wary of him, and their suspicion extended to encompass Leslie.

Although Leslie was always in the top stream, he never did more than enough work to get by. School was a place to have a lark, meet your friends and get the boring lessons over as soon as possible.

There was plenty of fun to be had out of school. Churchill Woods, now cut down, backed on to the estate and was the favourite hang-out for the loose gang of about fifteen boys from the estate who kicked around together. Often two or three of them would 'hop the wag' – play truant – from school and bunk off to the woods all day. They played with catapults, lit fires and made dens in a cave. There was a silver birch in the middle of the woods, with a worn dirt track round it where the boys raced their bikes. The most serious trouble they got into was smashing the lights in lamp-posts in stone-throwing contests. If ever they were pursued by the local bobby they would run round the back of St Mary Cray station and escape into the woods there.

Endless, unresolved games of football would be played on the green. Every Saturday morning one or two of the fathers would turn out, and the games would be more orderly. One of the fathers, an ex-commando, was a hit with all the kids for organizing boxing contests on the green.

When the Granthams moved to the estate, building work was in progress on the Seven Stiles public house, which would become the hub of all the estate's activities. A night watchman, Les Cracknell, was employed to guard the site: playing tricks on Les was good sport for the local kids, who terrorized him.

But there was better sport to be had when the Seven Stiles opened. The first landlord was Harry Huggett, who ran the pub with his wife Ada. The grand opening was a big affair: Jack Warner, one of the top TV and radio stars of the day, famous as Dixon of Dock Green, carried out the official opening ceremony. He had starred in one of the earliest soaps about a family called the Huggetts, so he was an appropriate choice.

Harry and Ada Huggett had no children of their own: Ada had suffered from tuberculosis of the hipbone. But they both liked youngsters, and the local kids soon found that they were friendly adversaries. Part of the building was an off-licence with a separate door from the pub. It sold chocolate, sweets and crips as well as alcoholic and soft drinks. Leslie – usually known as Les – and his mates soon learned that if they crowded in there with a couple of pennies to spend between them, they could confuse Harry Huggett enough to walk out with far more than they paid for. They also discovered how to open the door without the bell ringing, so that they could help themselves to sweets and chocolates before he realized they were in there.

When Harry got fed up with their pilfering he would ban them all from the off-licence – but the ban never lasted long. During the bans they would turn their attentions to the Fourbuoys newspaper and sweet shop, just across the road from the Seven Stiles. There they would try their usual tactic of crowding in to confuse the shop staff, buying something small and retreating with lots of unpaid for sweets and chocolates.

Round the back of the pub there was an old greengrocer's stall; nobody can remember where it came from or why it was there. But the boys used it for endless games of pontoon, gambling for halfpennies – or matches if they were all skint. Harry Huggett stored empty soda siphons round there, and many times the boys would take one or two and go round to the front of the pub to claim the deposit back on them.

Round the back of the pub Harry kept an old 1930s car, a wreck which fascinated the boys. It had running boards along the side, and they played gangsters on it, vying to be Al Capone and shooting each other with imaginary machine guns. He also had an old blue and white Hillman, which the boys used to be paid to clean. As a reward he would allow them into the public bar to drink Ribena and play darts – until Ada Huggett saw them and chased them out. Sometimes Harry would give them unofficial driving lessons round the pub car park.

As far as the Huggetts were concerned, Les was again living in the shadow of his big brother John – but not in the same way that their teachers saw them. All the Grantham boys were tall and strong for their age, but John was the tallest. By the time he was fourteen he was passing for eighteen and helping behind the bar at the Seven Stiles, where Ada and Harry worshipped him as if he had been their own son. As far as they were concerned, John could do no wrong. Les was John's younger brother, and as a result he was granted some special privileges: he was helping clear up the glasses before he was fifteen.

John was virtually managing the pub for the Huggetts by then, although he was doing a printing apprenticeship at the same time. His father, of course, had connections with the printing industry going back before the war, and Wally's brother Terry Grantham, who today lives in Croydon, was also working as a bookbinder. Between them they had managed to secure John a coveted six-year apprenticeship.

Talking to other residents of the Tillingbourne Green estate today, it is John Grantham who is most remembered of the whole family. Although Wally went to the Seven Stiles every Sunday lunchtime, he wasn't a weekday regular – he was rarely home from work before eight in the evening. Anne did not drink at the pub, but bought her cigarettes there every day.

The family are mostly remembered for how smart they were. Wally was every inch the old soldier, and the three boys were straight-backed, tall, good-looking and always well-dressed. But those who knew them well spotted something else in common: Wally and Anne are both witty, and their children have all inherited their sharp sense of humour. But as a family at this time they kept to themselves, not making more than casual friends on the estate. John, spending all his free time at the Seven Stiles, became well known to young and old alike on Tillingbourne Green.

Anne Grantham worked part-time as an auxiliary nurse, and later worked full-time on night duty. Wally had his war disability pension as well as his salary, so the Granthams were comparatively well off. They were rare among the estate's residents because they had a holiday every summer: Wally booked self-catering apartments in Clacton, Margate or Hastings. And on other days during the summer holidays the children would catch a train to Bickley, where they would swim or go apple scrumping.

Angela, the only girl, found that as a small child she played most with Philip, her younger brother. They would run errands for their mother together, and go hand in hand to pay the electricity bill at the showrooms. But in her teens she became much closer to Les: they went to the same school and he was a protective older brother to her. She remembers John as the patient older brother who spent a whole day teaching her how to tie her shoelaces – which Les would never have done. But Les, on the other hand, was the one who allowed her to join in the boys' games. When they had a tent in the garden and she made the jam sandwiches and lemonade, it was Les who agreed with her that it was unfair not to let her play in the tent. Philip passed his eleven-plus and went to Bromley Grammar School, where he eventually became head boy. His more studious life cut him off from his brothers and sister, and he became a loner within the family.

For Les, in those years, the most strenuous intellectual activity in which he voluntarily took part was to spend an afternoon with a bag of doughnuts and the *Beano* or the *Dandy* (an intellectual pursuit that survived into his army days), or to watch Norman Wisdom films on telly. He loved horror movies – Dracula, Frankenstein and other X-rated food of nightmares. Because they were tall, both he and John were able to get into these films under age, and from the age of thirteen he was a regular at the cinemas in Bromley or Orpington. His other great love was animals: he kept budgerigars and bred mice. The family dog, Butch, a cross between bulldog and labrador, didn't last long. It was a very excitable creature with a tendency to bite and, when it bit a passer-by it had to be put down. The whole family was upset.

With four children in the house, it was a noisy, often quarrelsome environment. Both Wally and Anne are by nature argumentative, and their marriage has never been peaceful or easy. Anne ran the household, but no one was in any doubt that Wally was the ultimate authority. Friends of Les remember his father chasing him the length of Tillingbourne Green and walloping him with his artificial arm.

While Wally was at work Les's friends would be welcome round at his house, where they would play cards and eat plates of chips that Anne would cook for them. All the local boys started smoking young – Les was hooked by the time he was thirteen. Anne accepted it, and would give them the money to get twenty Weights between them. But when the time for Wally's return from work approached, the other kids would slope away.

'We didn't hang around if he was about,' says Dave Caulfield, now a successful builder, who was one of Les's mates from the estate.

There was constant rivalry between Les and John, his

older brother. John, by nature gentle and kind, un-
wittingly overshadowed Leslie simply by being taller,
better-looking and more successful with girls. As Les
grew older his ambition was always to steal John's
girlfriends.

At school both the Grantham boys were in constant
trouble. Angela remembers her first day at Herne's
Rise, when the teacher walked into the classroom and
said: 'Which one is Grantham? Stand up.' From then
on she felt that her school career was blighted by the
reputations of her two older brothers. Both John and
Leslie regularly played truant, sometimes disappearing
for a week at a time to go fruit picking. Angela, too,
would play truant, but only for the odd day – and in
her case it was usually because she was exhausted by
the amount of housework she had to do while her
mother, working nights, was asleep.

Although the headmaster at Herne's Rise was
George Fawcett it was his deputy, 'Daddy' Day, who
terrorized the tough kids. He was aided by a
metalwork teacher with a ferocious reputation, Mr
Scali.

'When you had the cane from one of those two, you
knew you'd had it,' says Robert Tugwell, then in the
same year as Les at school, now a Civil Servant and
battling against multiple sclerosis.

Smoking was probably the most common offence,
and John and Les were marked men. 'The staff were
out to get us. They would pass half a dozen boys who
had been smoking and then pick on us,' says John,
'Les would rebel against it. And when they caned him
he would refuse to cry, which annoyed them.'

Some old air-raid shelters in the school grounds
became the usual hide-outs for the smokers, and
occasionally there would be a bit of smooching with
one of the girls going on there, too. On one occasion
the air- raid shelters were deliberately set on fire: the

culprits were never caught, but Les's name was one of three prime suspects.

At lunchtime Les and his pals would take their pick of the bikes in the bike shed, and ride off either to one of the pubs in the area where they could slip in under age, or to the local shops. The bikes would always be returned.

One old schoolmate, Jimmy Deighton, describes Les as 'The sort of lad who couldn't walk along a corridor without shoving or pushing someone, or tripping someone up. He was always making trouble in a minor sort of way. If there were twenty kids walking in an orderly fashion and one was scuffing, bobbing and weaving about in the line, you could guarantee it would be Les.

'We had a set of monkey bars at the school – you could pull yourself along on your hands. But if Les came up behind he'd jump up and put his hands over yours. You couldn't get off and your hands would hurt and your arms ache.

'When he was about thirteen he got into a fight with another lad who was wearing a ring, and the ring cut Les's face. For years afterwards he had a tiny scar. When we were a bit older, about fifteen, we all used to wear Chelsea boots with Cuban heels, and Les used to use the heel as a weapon.'

But despite these tricks, Les was popular. He treated girls the same as boys, which meant he was well liked by them, too, and he charmed most of his teachers into forgiving him for undone homework. Jimmy Deighton, who held the record for having the cane the most times, would often see Les in the queue outside the headmaster's study, waiting to be caned – mostly for playing truant or giving cheek. One particular teacher, who taught Religious Instruction, was an easy target for unfeeling young boys, and Les was among several who reduced him to tears.

But Jimmy and other friends remember that Les was also good at avoiding being the one to be caned. 'He had a knack for stopping messing about just at the right moment, leaving someone else to carry the can for him,' says Jimmy.

His sister Angela says, 'I've known Les take the cane when it wasn't his fault without turning a hair, and I've known him leave others to take the blame for him. It all depended how it suited Les.'

And although he often stirred others up to fight, he would avoid fighting himself if he could. 'He picked on me once too often and I took a pob at him,' says Jimmy Deighton. 'He didn't run away or anything, but I beat him in the fight, even though I was a year younger. I think he thought I was quiet, and therefore an easy target. He could be quite aggressive, but I saw him come unstuck a few times by taking on a fight with someone who could sort him out.'

When he was thirteen and a half Leslie joined Anglesey Road Army Cadets, where he was joined a year later by Jimmy Deighton, who says: 'We loved it – dressing up in uniform. Les was a first-class shot with a rifle – he always got top marks on the rifle range. They used to make us march up and down in front of mirrors and salute ourselves. Les really loved it. We used to strip down a Bren gun. We thought we were really something. But it was the uniform that Les liked most.'

One night while they were at cadets someone set fire to Jimmy Deighton's new jacket, bought for him by his mum only the day before. 'It was burned to smithereens while we were out on drill. I didn't half cop something when I got home.'

Once again, no culprit was found.

All the Grantham children were encouraged to work hard, and they all took part-time jobs. Apart from his fruit picking and helping out at the pub, by the time Les was eleven he was getting up at 3 a.m. on Saturday mornings to help on the Tip Top bread vans, delivering bread from the local Sunblest bakery down to the coastal towns of Bexhill and Eastbourne, and returning home about 5 p.m. with 12s 6d (62½p) for a day's hard work. He also did deliveries for a local butcher and he helped on a milk round.

'Money was always important to Les,' says Angela, 'and clothes. When he was little he looked like the wreck of the Hesperus, but when he became a teenager he smartened himself up. He always wanted to be the best dressed and have the most money in his pocket. We would often have boys knocking on our door saying Les owed them money, or fathers would come round and say Les had agreed to buy something from their sons and had never handed over the money. Dad used to go mad, but he always had to pay up. Les had a way of getting things out of mum and dad. Whatever he wanted, he got. If he wanted a camera, dad would grumble but Les would get it. He and John got far more than me and Philip: Dad never seemed to even notice Philip, and I was the one expected to do all the house-work. I had a much worse childhood than Leslie, but he's the one with the chip on his shoulder.'

Les became a teenager just at the start of the sixties, before the decade of decadence had begun to swing. But it was an exciting time for youngsters everywhere, with Elvis Presley, Adam Faith and the Everly Brothers dominating the charts. Les and his older brother Johnny were constantly told that they looked like Cliff Richard, and Johnny was also compared to Elvis Presley. They both enjoyed the comparisons.

'Johnny had all the latest fashions – winkle pickers, the lot. He had jet-black hair sleeked back, but he was charming, and all the girls fancied him like mad. Les looked good – always very mod, very fashionable – but Johnny was the outstandingly good-looking one,' says Robert Tugwell.

All the kids on the Tillingbourne Green estate were suddenly into pop music in a big way, especially after the Beatles exploded on to the scene just after Les's sixteenth birthday.

'We all wanted to be the Beatles or Dave Clark,' says Dave Caulfield, who remembers having a set of drums which drove the neighbours mad. 'Les had a tea chest that he made into a double bass. We used to all gather on the green and kid ourselves we were playing jazz.'

Jack Hitchcock, one of the regulars at the Seven Stiles, remembers Les well: 'When he was twelve or thirteen he used to hang around the doors of the Seven Stiles, cadging money or drinks from anyone who looked like a sucker. One day my wife and me and two other couples were having a bit of a party – the women would make some sandwiches and the men would bring some drink back from the pub. We did it regular. And Les turned up on the doorstep, with a tea chest with a broom handle through it. He said Rose, my wife, had told him he could come and play. He stood in the bay window with it and played it all night – he had us up dancing, the lot. He was really enjoying entertaining everyone.

'Then other times he'd play pontoon with us, and con us with his cleverness. He was always working, making money. One night in the pub him and a couple of mates tried to nick a hot sausage when the landlord was serving in the off-licence – but it was too hot and they dropped it into someone's beer. The bloke pulled it out, put it back on the hot tray and drank his beer. The kids couldn't stop laughing when an old lady came in and bought that sausage.

'He always looked smart. He lived with a comb in his back pocket.'

'A real little smoothie,' is how Robert Tugwell describes him.

'He was a real flash dresser, new clothes every five

minutes. We never knew how he could afford them,'
says Jimmy Deighton.

Ada Huggett, the landlady of the Seven Stiles, remembers him as the life and soul of any group, but
quiet when he was on his own. He enjoyed dancing,
and would prance around the juke-box on his own,
quite carried away with his own performance.

When the mods and rockers confrontations shook
Britain in 1963, Les was firmly on the side of the mods.
His hair was modishly long, he wore a mohair suit, and
when other kids were running around in sneakers he
always wore highly polished shoes. As they grew older,
the lads in the gang spent less time down in the woods
and more time hanging around on the wall outside the
Seven Stiles. For a few months Les owned a Vespa
scooter, paid for after he started work, and they would
spend hours cruising up and down the road on it. The
local girls would find excuses to walk backwards and
forwards past them, sometimes making four trips to the
shops when one would have done.

'We'd have our black ski pants, suede jackets and
hush puppies on. We were all mods, too,' says Sandra
Ward, who was Sandra Chandler in those days. 'All the
boys had Beatle haircuts. Les was always one of the
best dressed, with really sharp suits. We'd all have lots
of eye make-up on, and our hair all sleek and long. I
can't remember Les with any one girl in particular. He
used to just fool around with the crowd. He was always
a joker, at school as well.

'In many ways he seemed shy. I think all his joking
was to cover up his shyness. I think he was a bit
frightened of girls.'

For many of the boys in the gang, fooling around
with the local girls was the nearest they got to sexual
experiences. But for some of the gang there was
another, much less coy, teacher. Living on the estate
was a married woman whose husband had left her. She

had two young children, and a willing and open attitude
to sharing her bed with the youths of the estate. Several
of them lost their virginity in her council house – and the
rest learned a lot of the practical details about sex from
their endless discussions and bragging about what they
had done.

She was nicknamed Ben Gunn, although the reason
why seems to have been lost in everybody's memory.
And for the price of a bag of raisins and some liquorice
root – the bribe to persuade her children to go out and
play – she would share her favours, while other boys
from the gang sat on the wall outside and giggled.

'Les was one of the lads that used to hear about her
exploits,' says Dave Caulfield. 'I was younger, so I only
sat on the wall!'

There were no regular, serious girlfriends for Les. His
brother John remembers him dating a girl for a few
months before he went into the army, but it wasn't a big
affair.

'Like me, he never asked girls out in a formal sort of
way. He'd just joke around with them, and very often
they'd do the asking,' says John. 'This girlfriend was the
only one I ever remember him bringing to the house. He
was nervous about it, and spent ages getting himself
ready.'

Angela says, 'He was a real lad with the girls – he
could have had the pick of the bunch. But Les only went
for one-night stands. He wasn't interested in emotional
attachments. John used to break girls' hearts – but he
never intended to. He always cared about them, and
didn't want to hurt them. Les couldn't have cared less.
There were always a couple of girls flitting around in the
background when Les was about, but he'd be pretty
ruthless about moving on from one to the next.

'He's always been attractive to women, long before he
was famous. But women have never meant a great deal
to him.'

CHAPTER 2

Lance Corporal Grantham

Leslie could not wait to leave Herne's Rise Secondary Modern behind him. He left at fifteen, then the legal school leaving age, without staying on for an extra year to take examinations.

He first found a job with Burroughs Wellcome, a large drug development and manufacturing company. He didn't enjoy the work: his brother John says he couldn't stand having to vaccinate horses. Within a few months he had left and was serving in a gents' outfitters, Meakers in Bromley High Street. But he knew that wasn't how he wanted to spend the rest of his life. He was restless, at a loose end.

His father wasn't satisfied with his choice of career, either. John was serving his printing apprenticeship, which would assure him of a safe, well-paid future. Philip was doing very well at grammar school (although he felt then – and would feel throughout his life – that this was despite his parents, not because of them). Angela was a sensible girl who would find work as a secretary when she left school. Leslie was the one to worry about, the one with no clear idea of where his life was going.

So it was with great relief that his parents heard that he wanted to join the army. For Leslie it was a means of getting away from the claustrophobic home atmosphere, where he still shared a bedroom with John – with whom he didn't always get on well. It was a way back into the uniform that he had enjoyed when going to army cadets, and it was a type of life he felt confident would suit him. But most of all, according to his sister Angela, it was a way out of his immediate problems. And those problems, as usual with Leslie, were over money. Money, and the lack of it, dominated his life. The constant stream of youths to whom he owed money had not dried up when he started work full time, and his main reason for joining up was to get away from them all.

For his father there was a strong sense of pride. Although it had been wartime, Wally had enjoyed his years with the Royal Fusiliers, where his strong personality had taken him quickly through the ranks. He felt the army could make a man of his second son, and as soon as Leslie voiced the possibility of an army career Wally keenly pushed him towards it.

So Leslie signed on when he was sixteen, joining up just as the last conscripts were finishing their enforced National Service. Many of his friends were amazed: they did not see how the rebellious schoolboy would conform in the ranks. They could not imagine the trendiest dresser of their crowd having his hair shorn and wearing uniform all day. Some of them believed his father had forced him into it, but Angela and John are sure that it was his own choice.

On the eve of his leaving for the army, Sandra Ward remembers her father and some of his friends – all of whom had seen military service during the war – getting Leslie drunk in the Seven Stiles and making him march up and down. It was the only time she – or anyone else in the Tillingbourne Green area – can remember Leslie the worse for drink.

Leslie enlisted with his father's old regiment, the Royal Fusiliers (City of London Regiment). An historic regiment, its origins go back to 1685 when King James II decided to increase his personal security by raising new regiments. The first of these was 'Our Royal Regiment of Fuzileers', named after a new-fangled musket called a fusil. The regiment was garrisoned in the Tower of London, where to this day the Fusiliers have their headquarters. They are one of the few regiments allowed by royal privilege 'to march through the City of London with drums beating and bayonets fixed'.

During the First World War David Ben Gurion, the father of modern Israel, served in one of the Jewish battalions of the regiment, and during the Second World War Eric Morley, of Miss World fame, was another member of the regiment.

In 1968, two years after Leslie Grantham left, the Royal Fusiliers regiment was grouped together with the Royal Northumberland Fusiliers, the Royal Warwickshire Fusiliers and the Lancashire Fusiliers to become the Royal Regiment of Fusiliers.

As the City of London regiment, when Leslie joined it the Royal Fusiliers was full of Cockney lads. Michael Caine had done his National Service with the regiment, and so had the Kray twins. Reggie and Ronnie Kray were already established as East London mobsters when they were called up, and they ran the barrack room in much the same way that they ran the East End: with bully boy tactics, and by surrounding themselves with other heavies. When they were arrested for going AWOL, the officer in charge of their military escort from East London back to their barracks remembers them demanding to be released from their handcuffs on Liverpool Street Station in order to say goodbye to their mother properly. Aware that if he granted their request he might never see them again, but that if he didn't he might not live to see them again, the officer reluctantly released them. To his surprise, a few minutes later their adored mother Violet walked back to him, escorting her sons.

When Leslie enlisted he was given the battery of medical and intelligence tests that any new recruit has.

His results were good, and he was selected to become a Junior Leader – instead of being sent for ordinary basic training he went to Oswestry, to the Army Junior Leaders' Training Base, where soldiers whom the army foresees as destined to become NCOs are given a special, intensive introduction to army life, which incorporates learning about leadership.

'Being a Junior Leader does not automatically mean that you will get a stripe, but it means that you will be looked at more closely when you join the regiment,' says a senior Royal Fusiliers officer. 'Put it this way – once you have completed the Junior Leader training you will shine among the rest of the men. Very few don't become NCOs.'

Wally now had another reason to be proud of his son, and he told his friends and colleagues all about his son's potential career in the army.

After his training in the Junior Leaders, Leslie joined the First Battalion of the Royal Fusiliers in West Germany (there was only one battalion of the regiment at the time). The battalion was divided into companies – Leslie was in B Company. Each company was subdivided into platoons, each with three sections of eight to ten men. The functions of the different companies varied, and depended obviously on how they would be deployed in time of war. In the Royal Fusiliers most were rifle, or fighting, companies. There was a Headquarters Company, which provided cooks, drivers and clerks; and there was a Support Company, which provided heavy weapon support for the rifle platoons. The latter was Leslie's company.

Within a very short time of leaving the Junior Leaders the career prophecy that took him to Oswestry was fulfilled and he became a lance corporal, the lowest ranking non-commissioned officer. With one stripe on his arm he gave his father even more cause to be proud of him. When he was home on leave he would walk into

30

the Seven Stiles looking every inch the career soldier: tall (six feet and half an inch), straight-backed and smart. The public image he presented was that he enjoyed the army, and his older brother Johnny believes to this day that, if things had not turned out the way they did, he would have stayed in the army and made a successful career for himself.

His sister Angela, less gullible, less naïvely devoted to Leslie, and by her own admission closer to him in personality, believes that her brother knew almost from signing on that he had made a mistake. The path to the top was too slow, too regimented for the Leslie she knew: an impatient, ambitious young man who would always cut corners to get where he wanted, and insisted on doing things his own way. Money, too, was a driving motivation in everything he did, and the army was not a generous paymaster.

Osnabrück, where Leslie Grantham joined his regiment, is, like most German cities, clean and well planned. It was bombed heavily during the war, when nearly 70 per cent of the city was destroyed. Of the seventy thousand houses there today, over fifty thousand were built or heavily renovated after the end of the war, so that the overall impression is of a modern, spacious city with a few historic buildings dotted among the new redbrick and glass. Yet it is really a very old city; founded by the Emperor Charlemagne in AD 807. The central areas are pedestrian precincts, with lots of stylish clothes shops and bigger and better department stores than in most British cities of comparable size. The people are tall and athletic: one in every four of the 150,000 inhabitants is a member of a sports club. It is an industrial city: iron-ore mining has been going on in the region since the Middle Ages, and gave birth to the prosperous steel industry on which Osnabrück's fortunes are still founded. The Volkswagen Scirocco is manufactured there, and it has huge paper mills.

The new Leslie Grantham, the one who emerged from prison in 1978, would be interested in the city's famous theatre, the Civic Theatre in Cathedral Square, an art nouveau monstrosity which runs its own repertory company. And there are also a youth theatre and an experimental theatre group working in Osnabrück.

But the Leslie Grantham who moved to Osnabrück to join the First Battalion of the Royal Fusiliers in 1965 would not have taken much interest in the flourishing cultural life of the city. Osnabrück was and still is the main base for the British Army of the Rhine, with ten thousand British troops living in and around the city. Like most expatriate groups, they have established their own areas of the town. Many soldiers will spend six years in Germany and return to England not speaking more than three or four words of German. They drink in the NAAFI and in a few local pubs and bars where English is the common language.

Although the price of a pint in the NAAFI is about half that in a bar, the attraction of spending free time away from barracks is to meet 'fräuleins', the bar girls who are the only Germans that many British soldiers ever speak to. So in the couple of days after 'pay parade', when the soldiers have their money, the local bars are crowded. Because of the trouble that drunken and fighting soldiers can cause, many bars and restaurants in the better parts of the city carry signs announcing that they are out of bounds to British troops.

In 1964 the flag flying over Belfast barracks in Sedanstrasse in the smart Westerberg area of the city was the dark blue and gold of the Royal Fusiliers. There were a thousand fusiliers based there, halfway through a six-year posting to Germany. Belfast barracks was then one of three huge British barracks in Osnabrück – one of them, Caprivi, has recently been closed down. Belfast is a gaunt, grey building. Just opposite the gate on Artillerystrasse is the St Luke garrison church, and next to that is a school for English children of service families, the Wellington First School. Further along the road is the Carlisle Club, run by the Church Army, where tea and coffee are served. Soldiers use it as a venue to meet English girls – the daughters of other servicemen – or as a place to sit and chat.

In 1965 B Company was housed in B Block in the barracks, with different platoons on each floor. Grantham's platoon, anti-tank, was on the top floor, with rifle and recce (reconnaissance) platoons on the floors below. As a lance corporal Grantham shared a room with just one other man, whereas the soldiers in his section were eight to a room, across the landing from him. The rooms were furnished very basically, with iron bedsteads and a locker for each man, where uniform and civvy clothes were hung in separate compartments. A small section of it could be locked, and in there soldiers kept their private possessions: letters, photographs and money. Each bed had a bed box, where sheets and blankets were folded and stored during the day. Army regulations in those days stated that they had to be folded in nine-inch square piles.

Off duty Grantham, as a lance corporal, would be able to use the junior NCOs' mess, usually called the corporals' mess, as well as the NAAFI. But often the corporals and sergeants (who had their own mess) would drink with the ordinary soldiers in the NAAFI. When Grantham was in the army the relationships between the lower ranks were by and large informal and friendly.

Not that there was anything cosy about it. The regular army was a hard life, and many of the men who joined up were hard cases. There was a bar just along the road from Belfast barracks that was regularly smashed up on Friday evenings, and on several

33

occasions there were battles there between the squaddies and the military police.

At the time that Grantham was in Belfast barracks, one fusilier in another block‾ regularly threatened to commit suicide by jumping from the top-floor window of the block house, and was just as regularly pulled down from the window ledge. Another soldier remembers how others, tired of the constant threats, eventually pushed him out.

'It wasn't high enough to kill him, but it certainly did him some damage. He ended up in hospital and we never saw him again after that. I don't recall anybody being riven by guilt,' says an ex-soldier who witnessed the incident.

Grantham was not popular with the men under him. He went by the book: a stickler for neatness and tidiness. While some men in his section found him friendly and funny – the Grantham sense of humour – there were others who thought he was a bully. John Moore, who is now working for British Rail as a guard, joined Grantham's section in 1965 as the youngest and rawest recruit – and he had a rough ride.

'It was easy, picking on me. I knew nothing. There were others he wouldn't have dared pick on, but I was easy meat. He gave me hell. I was on charge practically every week, usually for insubordination.' John Moore admits that the more Grantham picked on him, the more he defied the NCO.

'Perhaps I asked for trouble. But my army record shows that after Grantham was arrested, my behaviour improved amazingly. The number of charges I was on dropped by 90 per cent. I didn't mind carrying out orders, I just objected to the petty ordering about he went in for, especially as he seemed so determined to pick on me. I had a stubborn streak that made me deliberately flout his authority, because it was being misused.

'I can remember one night when we had to go out on standby. It was to test how ready we would be in time of war. We had to get to a certain destination by a certain time. We got back to the barracks and everyone got bedded down and he ordered me out of bed to take all the weapons down and clean them. I saw it as victimization, but in an army situation you can't do anything about it.

'He once put me on such a silly charge that even the officer who heard the charge pulled a face and gave me a very small fine. But in army terms he was obviously efficient, and the sergeant-major over us treated him like a blue-eyed boy, thought the sun shone out of him.

'He wasn't a hard man. You are talking really hard men in a regiment like that. He wasn't one who got involved in fights at all. He just pulled rank if he ever had a grievance against anybody.'

Since Leslie's time in the army the number of petty offences for which soldiers can be put on charges has been considerably reduced, and the overall professionalism of the army has increased. Today, a sergeant expects to hear charges against soldiers only once or at the most twice a week, whereas in the 1960s it could have been as often as twice a day. Then, soldiers could be charged for being five minutes late getting out of bed; today, as long as they are on parade on time and satisfactorily turned out, it is up to them how they achieve it.

Les's interest in clothes continued. Among his civilian clothes he had two suits – a rarity among generally broke soldiers and a fact which, coupled with his address in Orpington, Kent, made others in his platoon assume he came from a moneyed background. He didn't court the impression, but he didn't deliberately disabuse anyone, either. Many of the men, joining the army from very poor backgrounds, had no civvy clothes at all, and most had only casual clothes.

All soldiers were issued with three uniforms: No. 1 dress is the smart blue formal uniform; No. 2 is khaki service dress, or battle dress; and the third uniform is denim fatigues, for working in. If the uniform issued was ill fitting it was possible to get a chit from a colour sergeant to have the uniform adapted by the company tailor, but the fit had to be very bad to justify this, and it usually involved only shortening trouser legs or taking in waistbands.

The tailors operated a nice sideline: they would adapt uniforms for any soldiers who were prepared to pay, measuring them to fit properly and turning out a good 'tailored' finish. 'Tailored uniforms' were highly prized. Les, naturally, had one. He kept his uniform well pressed, and his civvy clothes were always high quality and well cared for. The army laundry is notorious, and Les would join with mates to take his clothes to a launderette or dry cleaners. Again, as with his life before the army, the word most commonly used to describe him by those who knew him at the time is 'smart', and the tailored uniform is one of the first things that those who served with him comment on.

Ironically, one of the other soldiers who remembers Les Grantham is mass murderer Dennis Nilsen, who was a cook with Army Catering Corps attached to the Fusiliers. Nilsen was sentenced to life in 1983 for killing sixteen young men, most of them homeless vagrants, butchering their bodies and flushing their remains down the lavatory of his north London flat.

'Our paths crossed from time to time because I worked in his mess and cooked his meals three times a day,' says Nilsen today from his cell in Wakefield Prison. 'He appeared the epitome of a rising military star, a model professional. He was always well turned out in uniform or a well-cut suit. He was smart, keen, alert, intelligent and his only discernible fault appeared to be that he had a reputation for being a bit "cocky" or "flash". He was, perhaps, a bit of a loner.'

Life in a peacetime army can be tedious. It revolves around drills, preparation for drills, and maintaining weapons. As a lance corporal, Grantham was second in command of his platoon, which meant that he would supervise others as they stripped and cleaned the anti-tank weapons. After 6.30 a.m. reveille, every man would have a 'block duty' to carry out: sweeping the stairs, cleaning the lavatories and so on. Again, Grantham would supervise. He would also be second in command when his platoon were on guard duty at night, which happened every fourteen days. Normally, he and the other soldiers would be free from 5 p.m. onwards, and they would be allowed out of barracks until one minute before midnight unless they had a late pass – but friends on guard duty would turn a blind eye to those who arrived back after midnight. Occasional weekends would be spent on twenty-four-hour guard duty.

Every year the battalion would spend six weeks at Sennelager in central Germany, the Aldershot plain of West Germany, where there was room for full-scale manoeuvres. In addition, each company would spend another two weeks there on smaller exercises. Weather conditions at Sennelager can vary from almost Arctic in the winter months to approaching desert conditions in a good summer, making it an ideal training area. In 1965, twenty years after the end of the war, the Queen reviewed her troops there, on the same parade ground that Adolf Hitler used to review his troops: Leslie Grantham was among the ten thousand paraded in front of her.

There would be other weeks of the year spent away from Belfast barracks, on 'adventurous training', an important part of any soldier's life. It would involve learning rock-climbing, ski-ing, parachuting, sailing and exploring, all while living under canvas. Grantham was never very fond of sport as a schoolboy, and was far too concerned about the creases in his trousers and his hairstyle to enjoy roughing it.

Plenty of bullying went on, and there were 'miniature mobs' of hard men who ruled the others. 'Bedrailing' was a common punishment for anyone who let their comrades down, or failed to observe the unwritten laws of the barracks. A loose rail (or several) would be taken from the iron bed frames, and the unlucky culprit beaten with it. Varying degrees of injury were sustained: one fusilier serving at the same time as Grantham was in hospital for weeks after a severe beating.

The mini-mob who were ruling B Block at Belfast barracks were a tough bunch. There were four or five of them, all hard men. One of the leaders, better educated and better spoken than most squaddies, was a charmer who rarely did his own dirty work. But they could all fight, and did if anyone refused to do what they wanted.

The rackets they ran were straightforward: protection for anyone who needed it badly enough to pay for it, and loan sharking. Army pay was a meagre 20DM a week (just under £2, significantly less than the average weekly wage of the time), and as in all barracks most soldiers were chronically and habitually broke. Grantham, paid more than them because of his rank, smoked, played cards and liked nice clothes: so even though he didn't drink as much as many of his mates, nor spend money on girls, he too was always short of cash. A brisk trade operated in NAAFI cigarette vouchers – every soldier was given an allowance of vouchers that were almost as valuable as currency.

The mob always had money, went to the best night-clubs in Osnabrück, and always had plenty of girlfriends. Barrack room life is a microcosm of life outside, and any newcomer who entered soon knew that these men were the winners. Anyone who crossed them paid a high price. Although bullying is today a much talked about feature of army life, and successful prosecutions have been brought against officers and soldiers who indulged in it, it has always been rife. Most squaddies who wanted a quiet life kept out of the way of the mob.

Les Grantham, desperate for money, did not. He ran up debts that he could not pay. He ended up owing a sum that would today seem trivial (300DM – about £27) but in those days represented several weeks' pay. He had no chance of paying it off.

He was frightened. Anyone who ran up against the mob was frightened. Other soldiers had been badly injured by them. There were rumours all around the barracks that they didn't content themselves with beating up their victims, but extended their violence to the victims' families back home when they were in England on leave – and even that they had connections with East End mobsters who were happy to oblige them by 'leaning' on families.

Leslie was very worried. He had joined the army to escape the pressure of home, to please his father and to gain some respect. He knew he would lose all this if his tormentors turned up on the doorstep in Tillingbourne Green demanding money with menaces; and he was actually frightened that his mother would be physically hurt.

When he couldn't pay his debt, four members of the gang carried out the first stage of their planned torture. They held him down while one of them branded his face with a red-hot iron. It left a livid red scar above his eyebrow and on his cheek. And he was warned: that was just the first instalment. If he could not find the money, there would be worse to come.

Tony McDermott, one of the gang who branded

Leslie, says, 'It was no more than he deserved. He had it coming to him. He owed money. And yes, I did brand him with a red-hot iron as well as threatening to kill him on several occasions.'

Against the background of these threats, Leslie went home on leave. His sister Angela was getting engaged and the whole family were celebrating with a party at home. Angela, seventeen at the time, was planning to marry Graham McNab, a clerk in a shipping company whom she had met at a dance just before she left school. By this time Angela was working as a switchboard operator. Graham and Leslie got on well, although John Grantham thought that Graham was too quiet and not exciting enough for his pretty sister. Good looks run in the family: all the Grantham children grew up to be attractive adults. Angela, although not tall like her brothers, is slim with large eyes and fine-boned features.

Leslie kept his problems from his family. He even bought an engagement present of a set of saucepans for Angela and Graham. 'We didn't have a clue he was short of money,' she says.

He asked John for a loan, but his brother wasn't able to help him out.

'I was a printing apprentice – I earned £2 10s a week [£2.50] and gave £1 of that to my mum. I paid nearly another £1 in fares – so there wasn't a lot left over. He didn't tell me he was desperate. Just asked in a casual sort of way.'

At the end of his two-week leave he travelled back to Germany, knowing that he could not pay his debt.

CHAPTER 3

Death in a Taxi

Because money is always in short supply in barracks, soldiers spend a lot of their time discussing how and where to get it. Leslie Grantham was no exception. The only factor that was different about him was his desperation, which gave him the determination to carry out one of the schemes he and his mates dreamed up. They talked about robbery, seeing it as a quick and easy way to solve their problems. And as soldiers they reckoned they could slip back into the anonymity of the barracks and never be detected: to the Germans, one British accent is much the same as any other, and at night with their faces hidden they believed they could get away unrecognized. They knew other soldiers who had done it, and the unwritten code of the barracks was that they all covered up for each other.

But Les didn't want to carry out his robbery plans alone. He asked a couple of his mates if they would help him 'roll a few Germans'. When one of them asked him who he intended to rob, he replied, 'Wait for a drunk to come out of a pub, or a taxi driver – the easy stuff.'

There had been an epidemic of robberies from taxi drivers across Germany for the last couple of years. German taxis do not have a glass partition separating the driver from his fare, and late at night it was relatively easy to threaten a driver and make off with his takings. Several drivers had been murdered in the pursuit of theft. Although no British soldiers had been implicated, it made big news across the country and was reported by British Forces newspapers and radio.

The other two soldiers decided not to go with Les. One of them said he preferred to go to bed, and the other 'bottled out' – decided not to go because he was afraid.

So on Saturday, 3 December 1966, at about 10.30 p.m., Les left the barracks alone. He had a gun that had been handed to him by another lance corporal who was working as an armoury storeman, and just 1.30DM, borrowed from the same man, in his pocket. Les left the camp by climbing the fence by the MRS – the military reception station, a sort of mini-hospital where soldiers with minor ailments were treated, and those returning from civilian hospitals were taken to convalesce.

The story of the Saturday night that changed his life and wrecked that of many others can be told in his own words, taken from the statement he gave nine days later to army investigators. The statement was kept, with others made by witnesses, in the German police file.

> I came back from roll call, saw Lance Corporal Norman Marks and said to him that I wanted to go out that night and asked him if he would come with me. He said 'No.' Then I said to him 'I want to go and change.' I asked him if he would give me an air pistol when I had changed.
>
> I changed into my blue suit and check raincoat. Then I went to look for him in his room. We went together to the armoury. He suggested I should take a 9mm revolver. But I said I wanted an air pistol.
>
> Marks pointed out that if I was going to hold somebody up with an air pistol it would be

spotted right away that it was not a real gun. Then I saw the 6mm pistol and said I would take that one. The magazine was already in the gun and I asked him to wait a minute – I wanted to go and get my gloves.

Marks stayed in the armoury. I got my gloves and went back down. Marks gave me the gun and some money for a drink. After I left Marks I jumped over the fence at the MRS. Then I went to the pub known as the Green Window. I bought a portion of chips and a beer. I spoke to Corporal Dempsey, Corporal Jasock and Corporal Reynolds.

I left the pub and went through the town, where I met this drunken German who I really wanted to rob. We went together to 10 Bremerstrasse and he asked me if I wanted to go in with him. I said 'No.' I left him and fifty to a hundred yards away I stopped a taxi.

I told the driver to take me to Albertstrasse. He drove there but stopped at Caprivi barracks. I said 'No, not here. Just go round the corner.' Then we drove round for about five minutes. He stopped in front of a house.

I pulled out the gun and asked him for money. He grabbed for the gun, and at the same time tried to open the door to get out of the car. He pushed me against the door, then I heard a click. He tried to grab my hand with his right hand and open the door with his left. He was trying to open the door and pull me after him. He shrieked and screamed.

I hit him twice with the gun on the side of the neck. Then the gun went off. He started gurgling and blood flowed from his face. He let go and I let the pistol drop inside the taxi. I tried to open the door from the inside but could not. As I tried to get out of the taxi it rolled backwards. I was afraid the whole time. I pulled on the handbrake and I tried to stop the taxi. Then I pulled down the window, grabbed the door handle and opened it from outside.

I ran away up the street. But as I ran it dawned on me that I had left the pistol behind. I went back to collect it. As I opened the door his head rolled from side to side. I picked up the gun from the floor, re-loaded and heard a sudden ping. I closed the door, ran up the street and turned right. I ran to the main road and kept running until I reached the barracks. As I ran away from the taxi I loaded the gun again. One or more bullets fell out.

As I got to the barracks, I spoke to Fusilier Abbot who was on guard at the gate. I said to him, 'You did not see me. And if anyone asks, I came back at 1 a.m.' Then I went to Marks' room, woke him and said that I wanted to see him downstairs. He got dressed and went with me to the armoury. When we got inside I got hold of him and said, 'Did you know there were bullets in that gun?' He said, 'Yes, why? Didn't you check?' I said, 'No, I didn't think there was anything in it.'

He took the gun from me and started to clean and oil it. He cleaned it and put it away and said if anyone asked about the gun, he would say he never gave it out. Then we locked up and went upstairs, where I washed my hands. After I washed my hands I asked what would happen if it was found out it was this gun. He said, 'I will simply say I do not know how it got out of the armoury. Anyone could get in because the lock was broken.'

Then he said to me that I should go to bed.
He said he would see me the next morning and
think something up. I went to bed and woke
up the following morning at about nine
o'clock. I saw Marks and said to him, 'Don't
forget, if they find out it was me, you are also
in it, because you gave me the gun and the
ammunition.' He said, 'Don't give me any
problems. I want to get home for Christmas.'

I was sitting in the classroom when Fusilier
Abbot came in and said a couple of taxi drivers
came while he was on guard duty. They were
asking about another taxi driver, and the duty
officer asked him if he had seen anyone come
in between 1 a.m. and 3 a.m. He said he had
not seen anyone. Another fusilier asked what
was up. And Abbot said he would find out.
Abbot then went out and the other fusilier
asked me if I knew anything. I said that I
knew. I also said that I was afraid and did not
know what to do. Then I told him everything.
He promised that he would not tell anyone.
And now that I had cleaned the gun, everything would be OK. He went to eat and I went
and got a cigarette. There were then only two
men in the room, Miles and Young.

Miles asked, 'Are you still going out
tonight?' I said, 'No, I am in enough trouble.'
I left the room and went to my room and laid
on the bed. Then I searched through my
locker and found there was blood on my suit
and on my coat. I went back and asked Miles
what he would do if I had bloodstained
clothes. He told me, 'Bury them. Bring them
down to the bunker.'

Then I went back to my room, laid on my
bed and fell asleep. Fusilier Winters came in

and asked if it would be OK with me if he could take my suit to the cleaners because he wanted to borrow it. I gave him the blue and grey mohair and said he could put it in the cleaners the following day.

The next night Marks came to me and said the SIB [the army's Special Investigations Branch] had just been and had taken the pistol. He told me to hide anything with blood on it. I went straight back to my room and cut up the suit and my coat and packed the stuff in a cardboard box. I covered everything with the *News of the World*.

Then I asked another fusilier if he would help me. We went together to Prestatyn barracks and found a gully. We put the stuff in and covered it with stones. I went back to the barracks and said to Marks that I had taken away the bloodstained clothes. He said, 'Good, now they won't be able to find any proof.' I said, 'Just remember who gave me the gun if they find out it was me.' He said I could rest assured that they would not find anything out from him.

That is everything apart from saying that I met the fusilier who helped me hide the clothes on Saturday, and he asked if I knew a reward had been offered. I told him I did not. I asked him if he was thinking of claiming it. He said he did not fink on anyone.

I would just like to add that at no time until the shooting did I know the gun was loaded.

That last sentence would become the most crucial in the whole statement, because at the court martial the whole of Leslie Grantham's defence would rest on it. Did he know the gun was loaded? Lance Corporal

Norman Marks, the armoury storeman who handed him the weapon, maintained that he did. But in his original statement to the SIB, Marks said there was no ammunition with the gun. He changed his statement twice over the few days after Grantham's arrest.

His original statement said:

> I am employed in the armoury of Support Company, 1st battalion Royal Fusiliers. Lance Corporal Grantham is an acquaintance of mine and I have known him since the end of 1963.
>
> Either on Thursday 1st December or Friday 2nd December 1966 Colour Sergeant Moore gave me a .22mm Walther to take care of in the armoury. After the Last Post on December 3rd, at 10 p.m. I spoke to Lance Corporal Grantham and he asked me if he could have a pistol from the armoury. When he asked me he was wearing a dark suit and a light-coloured coat. I asked him why he wanted a pistol and he said he wanted it to go out and get some money. But he did not tell me what he was going to do with it.
>
> I then went with Lance Corporal Grantham down to the armoury and opened the door. I opened the security door and took the .22 Walther pistol out.
>
> I gave Lance Corporal Grantham this pistol and he said he would bring it back later. I also gave him a magazine for the gun, but there was no ammunition in the weapons store. On the 4th December between 1.30 and 2 a.m. Lance Corporal Grantham came back to my barrack room and woke me up. I got dressed and we then went down to the armoury.
>
> It was then I noticed Lance Corporal

Grantham's hands had blood on them, and he had bloodstains on his forehead. But I did not see any blood on his clothing. When he handed back the .22 Walther I also noticed there was blood on the gun. I asked Lance Corporal Grantham what he had done and he said he had hit someone with it. I gave him a flannel towel and he cleaned the gun with it. After he cleaned the gun I lightly oiled it. But I did not clean the bore.

The magazine at this time was not in the gun, and I put the pistol and the magazine on the proper shelves and closed the security cupboard. Grantham and I then left the armoury and I locked the door. There was nothing more said about how the blood got on to the gun. On December 5th at around 19.30 hours I gave a member of the Royal Military Police the .22 Walther pistol and the two magazines. This was the same pistol that I gave Lance Corporal Grantham and allowed him to take out of the store.

Since the time Lance Corporal Grantham handed the .22 Walther back to me, he had not spoken to me. Later in the week I asked him if he had shot the taxi driver in Osnabrück. He answered yes, and laughed in a funny kind of way.

When I saw the blood on the Walther pistol it was still pretty fresh, if not wet. Today, on December 10th, I was shown some torn clothes and I can positively say that the navy coloured suit was the suit that Lance Corporal Grantham was wearing when he picked up the .22 pistol from the armoury, and was the same suit he wore when he brought it back. The coat I have identified as the same

coat Lance Corporal Grantham wore at the
time.

Later the same day, Lance Corporal Marks made a
second statement, this one crucially different on the
question of ammunition:

> When I gave Lance Corporal Grantham the
> .22 pistol he asked me for ammunition for the
> gun. I gave him five or six bullets. It was loose
> ammunition, and in my presence he loaded it
> into the magazine.
>
> I remember saying to him 'Why do you need
> it?' He said 'Just in case.'
>
> When he brought the pistol back in the early
> hours of the following morning and we went
> back to the armoury, I saw the magazine lying
> on the table. It was empty. I asked him where
> the ammunition was and he said, 'I fired it into
> a wood.'
>
> At this time he also said to me that he had
> hit a drunken man with it in the head, and this
> was the reason the blood came to be on the
> gun.
>
> At the same time I gave Lance Corporal
> Grantham the pistol. I loaned him 1.30DM in
> small change. He said he wanted it to buy a
> drink.

In a third statement Lance Corporal Marks said:

> I lay awake thinking what Grantham had said
> to me. It occurred to me that Grantham could
> have shot somebody. I went to his room at
> about four o'clock. He was alone. I asked him
> straight out if he had shot someone the pre-
> vious evening. He said he got into a taxi and

held up the driver. The taxi driver went for him, and he had shot him. Lance Corporal Grantham told me to tell no one that I had given him the .22 pistol that evening. If this got out we would both end up in prison for a long time.

At the same time Lance Corporal Grantham told me he had got rid of his clothes.

On Monday December 5th I told him that the SIB [Special Investigations Branch] had collected the .22 pistol from the armoury and he said to tell no one that I had loaned him the gun. During the week I saw Lance Corporal Grantham again. He laughed and joked with other soldiers in the unit about the murder of the taxi driver.

The laughing is corroborated by the fusilier who helped Les dispose of his bloodstained clothing. At the court martial this soldier would tell the court that Leslie Grantham was laughing when he told him that he had shot the driver to get money.

Unlike other ex-soldiers who knew Leslie Grantham well, and knew that he had committed the crime, this ex-fusilier has been willing to relive his memories of the nine days in December 1966 – but only on condition that he is not named. After being named in the *Sun* as 'the mate who gave him away' he and his family received hate mail and vicious telephone calls. Having moved to a new address and a new area he does not wish to go through all that again, and it was only after an undertaking not to reveal his name that he was willing to talk.

He was a boxer in the battalion boxing team, and he joined B Company while Les was home on leave attending his sister Angela's engagement party. It was only when he returned that they became acquainted –

just a few days before the murder. Because they both came from the same area of Kent they had plenty to talk about, and the boxer found him a likeable enough companion, although he was aware that Les was not popular because he owed money.

The boxer, nicknamed Titch because he was a flyweight, came back on Sunday evening. It was quiet in the barracks, as most soldiers had gone out. He went upstairs to find another boxer, a friend, and passed the open door to Leslie Grantham's room. Les was on the bed, cutting up his bloodstained clothes. The main light was not on, but a small bed light was on. The boxer immediately assumed he had been in a fight: England's recent victory in the World Cup against West Germany had led to a heavy spate of scraps between soldiers and local youths. It was quite common for soldiers to arrive back in barracks covered in mud and blood.

'He said "I've shot a taxi driver." I thought he was winding me up. He said, "I have, I've done it." Then I panicked. There was a funny look on his face, I thought he looked like some sort of nutter. He said, "You aren't going to grass on me, are you? Where can I hide these?"'

The boxer says he suggested stuffing them in a drainpipe near an old barracks building, which he knew about because it was close to the gymnasium. They went together – Les wearing plimsolls and casual clothes – out of the main gate, where they turned right and then left. There was a guard on the gate, but two soldiers going in and out together was unremarkable.

'My stomach was in knots, I was going to pieces. We lifted a cover and then stuffed them in a drain, and put stones on top. He was mumbling on about the cab all the time. He told me the whole story. I thought, "Blimey, I don't want to be involved in this."'

The following week the young boxer found it impossible to concentrate on his sport. He was nervous, upset, distracted. He kept out of Leslie Grantham's way, but whenever he did see him he was surprised how cool he was. By the next weekend Titch was so distraught that another member of the boxing team, who lived in married quarters, took him home with him. As they watched television together an appeal was broadcast for information about the killing, and photographs of the dead man's widow and child were shown. His anxiety was visible, and when the older, married boxer questioned him about what was wrong he told the whole story. He was worried because he believed he was an accessory to murder, having helped dispose of the clothing. But most of all he was upset about the harsh reality of the crime: how it had robbed a family of its father and breadwinner.

'After I told the other boxer he came with me over to the SIB. I didn't need much convincing that I had to make a clean breast of it. I didn't want to land a mate in trouble, but I felt that what he had done to that family was more important.

'I wasn't the only one who knew – there must have been a few others having a bad time with their consciences that week.'

The following day, Leslie Grantham was arrested.

CHAPTER 4

Felix Reese – Victim

Felix Reese was one of a big family. He was the youngest of eight children, four of them half-brothers and sisters because his mother Alviene had been widowed and remarried. His father, Heinrich, was a railway worker in Osnabrück, where there is a massive goods station as well as a large passenger station. It was a close, hard-working family but money was obviously scarce. Things were a little easier for Felix than for his brothers and sisters, because he was the youngest, and by the time he was growing up some of the older ones were already working.

Felix was the apple of his mother's eye. He could do no wrong, and one of his older sisters worried that, with so many doting older brothers and sisters, he would grow up lazy and spoilt. But his father was quite strict, and when young Felix left school at sixteen he soon found work as a delivery boy. He had one ambition: to drive his own van. As soon as he was eighteen – the legal age for learning to drive in Germany – he took lessons and passed his driving test. By the time he was twenty he had a job driving a van delivering coffee to shops and restaurants all around the city.

Liesel Reese, born Weilage, was two years younger than her husband. Her birthplace was Bersenbrück, a pretty village famous for its ancient Cistercian monastery, about twenty miles north of Osnabrück. When she was thirteen her father Heinrich, a builder, brought her and her mother, Ella, and younger sister

Helga to live in Voxtrup, an outer suburb of Osnabrück. There was more work for him in the city than in the countryside.

Liesel grew into a pretty, dark-haired, shy girl. She made friends with girls easily, but was very reserved with boys. When she left school she found a job in a weaving mill.

It was on a trip to the Wellmann swimming pool in the summer of 1956, when she was eighteen, that Liesel met Felix. She was with a group of girls, most of them friends from work. There was another group of boys, and there was the usual larking around that goes on when youngsters meet. They were splashing each other, and the daring girls were pushing the boys into the pool. Liesel was quieter than the others, and that was what struck Felix about her straightaway. He was shy, too, with girls – although he was in the forefront of the fun with the other boys. The two of them exchanged glances but did not speak directly to each other.

Arrangements were made between the two groups of youngsters to be at the pool the same time on another day, and this time Felix spoke to Liesel. He bought her an ice cream, and they spent the whole time talking together, not swimming. From then on, Liesel and Felix were a couple.

Felix was the same height as Liesel – five feet five inches. But he was not self-conscious about being short. He was quite strongly built, with a thatch of dark brown hair. He was already wearing glasses for reading and close work, and because of this he had not had to do National Service – conscription still exists in West Germany to this day.

'I had had no other boyfriend, and I don't think Felix had any serious girlfriends before me. We just knew straightaway that we liked each other, and then being with him just felt so right,' says Liesel.

For two years the young couple went out together.
Liesel met Felix's family, Felix met hers. They went to
the cinema, and they loved dancing. They were both
good ballroom dancers, and the cha-cha was the latest
craze: they loved it. Jiving and rock and roll were just
starting, but Felix and Liesel were more traditional. In
the summer months they went for picnics with friends,
and they made many nostalgic trips back to the
Wellmann swimming pool.

When she was nineteen Liesel's family moved. Her
mother and father bought their own home in the
Schinkel area of Osnabrück. Schinkel is much further
in towards the city centre than Voxtrup, and is considered to be a poor area. There is a large industrial
estate close by, and many of the flats and houses in the
area are lived in by *Gastarbeiter* – the foreigners,
mainly Turks, who live in Germany and do the dirty,
menial jobs that the prosperous natives don't want to
do.

If Schinkel is poor, then by British standards it does
not look so. The houses are modern and detached, with
neat gardens around them. The streets are clean. Most
of the houses are sub-divided into flats, and many of
them are privately rented. But the general appearance
of the place would make it a prosperous suburb of a
British city.

Mortgages are expensive in Germany, so when
Liesel's parents bought their home they rented out the
upstairs as a flat. Downstairs they lived in two
bedrooms, a living room and a kitchen.

When she was twenty, Liesel became engaged to
Felix. Following German tradition, he gave her a plain
gold band ring. Her parents were delighted, and from
that day on both Felix and Liesel saved every penny
they could towards their wedding, which took place on
8 October 1960, at St Paul's Protestant church in
Schinkel.

Liesel wore a long white wedding dress with a train, and carried fresh flowers. There was no honeymoon – they were not common at the time in Germany, and the young couple needed all the money they could save to set up their home. But there was a large party at the local Witte's pub, which has a hall attached to it. Today it is a billiards hall, but in 1960 it was hired out, and Liesel's parents paid for a dance band and food and drink for sixty guests, most of them family.

'It was a lovely day. The weather was good – not too warm but at least dry. We were so happy. Everything was working out for us,' says Liesel.

The tenants in the flat above her parents had left, so Felix and Liesel moved in, paying money to her parents to help with the mortgage payments on the building. Their flat was even smaller than the one downstairs: the living room was only about twelve feet square, and the smaller of the two bedrooms was no more than a boxroom. From the living room a door led on to a balcony over part of the downstairs flat. But Liesel and her new husband were delighted: they had their own home, and they had saved enough money to buy all the essential furniture they needed to start married life.

Liesel went back to work in the weaving factory after the wedding, but left six months later when she was expecting a baby. Her daughter Kirsten was born on 23 September 1961, almost a year after their marriage. Both Felix and Liesel were delighted.

'The smile did not leave Felix's face for days. He was always a man to smile and sing a lot, but after Kirsten was born he never stopped! He bored everybody at his work talking about Kirsten all the time. They used to joke about it when I met any of them,' says Liesel.

He christened Kirsten, 'my little nose bear' when she was tiny, and that remained her nickname until his death. 'But he was really the "bear" in the family. He couldn't pass either of us without giving us a big hug,' says Liesel.

Money was obviously tighter, because Liesel had stopped work and there was a baby to feed and clothe – and Felix wanted the best of everything for his plump little daughter. He was also saving to buy a bigger house for his family. But they were very happy. Kirsten's earliest memory of her father is of him running up and down the hallway of their flat in his long underwear, roaring and pretending to be a gorilla.

'I was upset about something and he was trying to make me laugh. I remember so little about Papa, but most of all I remember him fooling around with me and laughing. He was always laughing.

'One day he was painting the outside of the house downstairs, and I was playing in the sandpit that he built me, with my friend Mariella who lived near us. Grandma called him to come in for coffee, and he left his paint and brushes outside. The neighbours' cat came into our garden, and Mariella and I picked up the brushes and painted it white. She held it by the tail while I daubed the paint on, then we ran away and hid. Papa came out and started painting again, but in a few minutes the neighbour came along carrying the cat and shouting. Papa took one look at the cat and he couldn't stop laughing. The more he laughed the more the neighbour shouted – she was furious, crying and shouting at the same time. He tried to tell me off later, but he was laughing too much to sound cross.'

Kirsten remembers her favourite ritual with Felix. On Sundays, while her mother was cooking the lunch, she would go for a 'walk' with her papa. 'The walk always ended at Marthe's bar, where Papa would sit me on a stool at the bar and give me some coins to put in a machine to get a handful of nuts. Sometimes he would give me a small glass of malt beer and a sausage –

Mama was not supposed to know, because she would think it would spoil my lunch.'

Frequently Felix would arrive home with sweets and presents for his daughter. He spoiled her terribly – and Liesel used to tell him off. 'Some days she would have been really naughty. She would hide whenever I wanted to take her out. So I would be cross with her – and then her papa would arrive home with presents. He worshipped her. She was quite plump from all the spoiling she got, from her papa and her grandmother and grandfather downstairs.'

Felix and Liesel wanted another child, but Felix was determined they should have a bigger home to live in first. He was determined to earn more money. So four years after Kirsten was born he decided to change his job from driving a coffee delivery van to becoming a taxi driver. Liesel was worried, and told him so. Germany was in the middle of a wave of violence, and taxi drivers were obvious targets for thugs trying to raise easy money. There had been several deaths of drivers already.

'He didn't tell me he was changing jobs – he just *did* it, because he knew I would be upset and try to persuade him not to. But he told me not to be afraid, and when I asked him if he was afraid he would just laugh and say nothing could happen to him. Whenever there was something in the paper about a driver being attacked I would beg him to go back to his old job, but he was happy driving the cab.'

Felix was driving for Georg Liekam, a cab owner who had expanded his business by buying another car and taking on other drivers. Georg's wife Marlise helped run the business, taking the bookings for the cabs.

'Felix was a lovely man, always friendly, hard-working and willing. We had been nervous about taking on another driver, but it worked so well with

Felix. He was always punctual, and he always laughed. We talked a lot about the other taxi murders and I always told him: give them the money. It is not worth losing your life for a few marks. He would just laugh and say it would never happen to him,' says Marlise Liekam.

For the year that Felix was driving the cab, everything seemed particularly good for him and Liesel. He was earning a lot more money – above the average German wage. He was able to save, and yet the family ate well and Kirsten always had new clothes. He worked shifts, sometimes days and sometimes nights, but because Kirsten was not yet at school the family could revolve around his hours.

'We would change our mealtimes to suit Felix's shifts. If he was on nights he would always have a good meal before he went, and we would eat early with him. He loved meat – lots of it. He had a big appetite.'

Newspaper headlines were screaming increasingly about the '*Taxi Morden*'. Georg and Marlise Liekam travelled to funerals for murdered taxi drivers in Bonn, Frankfurt and Hamburg; the deaths were occurring with sickening regularity, and as a mark of respect drivers from all over the country would flock to the funerals with black flags attached to the aerials of their cabs. In the month before the murder of Felix Reese there were four other murders: a twenty-five-year-old driver was stabbed to death in Munich on 12 November; a forty-four-year-old was shot in Frankfurt just four days later. Four days after that a forty-one-year-old in Würzburg was stabbed to death, and on 28 November a fifty-four-year-old driver was beaten to death in Berlin. None of the murders was solved. There had been no killings of taxi men in Osnabrück, but a local driver had been badly injured when a screwdriver had been thrust into the back of his neck.

Felix and Liesel used to go to their local *Schützenfest*,

or shooting festival. The *Schützenfest* is a tradition all over Germany, where shooting is a major form of re-creation. In Osnabrück alone there are fourteen shooting ranges. Each district has its own club, which once a year holds a festival. One of the club members is chosen *Schützenkönig*, or Shooting King, for the occasion. The festival lasts all day and all night, and is really just a good excuse for everyone to drink a lot and have a very good time. There is a band playing traditional oompah-pah-oompah-pah music, dancing, singing and speeches. The King has his own table and invites his own guests; everyone wears medals; and the men put on their green shooting breeches and jackets, with feathers in their hats.

It was Felix's most treasured ambition to be the *Schützenkönig* one day. He would tell Liesel that she was his Queen, and one day he would make her a real Queen, if only for one day.

Each club also organizes social events throughout the year, paid for out of money saved regularly by members, who each have their own little savings box at their local pub. Felix and Liesel were members of the Allgemeine Schützenverein in Schinkel, and Felix's savings box was at Marthe's bar in Zum Heide Krug, not half a mile from their home.

Felix enjoyed the social events more than the shooting, although he always took part in his club's shooting competitions, using the club's guns. It was rare for any member of a club to have his own guns.

It was because of the shooting club that Felix was working on the night of Saturday, 3 December 1966. He and Georg's other driver took it in turns to work the Saturday late shift, a busy time for taxis. It should have been the other driver's turn, but Felix asked if he could change shifts because the following Saturday he and Liesel wanted to go to a dinner-dance run by the club. Georg agreed.

Felix left for work at 6 p.m. after a dinner of veal and fried potatoes. He told Liesel that he had been lucky changing shifts, because the weather was unusually fine for the time of year: cold, but clear and dry. The following week, he said, it would probably be wet and might even be icy. He kissed both Liesel and Kirsten goodbye, and went out singing. He climbed into the black Mercedes, taxi number 46, registration number OS-Y-21, owned by Georg Liekam, and drove off. That was the last time his wife and daughter ever saw him.

He carried thirteen other passengers before he picked up Leslie Grantham in the early hours of the morning. At 10.30 p.m. he was at the railway station, where he had a chat with another taxi driver, Ursula Albrecht. She was his last colleague to see him alive.

'As usual he talked about Kirsten. He always talked about Kirsten,' says Frau Albrecht, who is still driving a taxi in Osnabrück.

Elsewhere in the city Manfred Wingerberg, a twenty- five-year-old student at Osnabrück's famous engineering college, arrived home at one o'clock on Sunday morning after an evening with friends. He had a room in a smart house in Albertstrasse, in the exclusive Westerberg district. Many of the local families rented out rooms to students and young working people, because the houses were large and expensive to run – today they would sell for the equivalent of £100,000 to £150,000. Manfred let himself in quietly, so as not to wake the landlord and his wife, and started to get undressed for bed. About ten minutes after arriving home he heard a noise in the street. He went to the window.

'I saw a black Mercedes with its back to the front of our neighbours' garden. The headlights were on but the engine was off, and I couldn't seek anything in the car.'

After a few moments in which nothing seemed to be happening, Manfred took some binoculars from a cupboard and switched off the light in the room he was in, so that he could see better. He saw a man run across the street and disappear from view. He got dressed again, and then went back to the window. The man had returned and was bending down near the driver's window.

'I took it he was looking in the car. I opened the window, and at the same time I heard a noise. The man stood up and ran away. I noticed it was about ten past one by my watch. I hurried down to the street. The headlights were still on, and there was one person in the car, leaning over the steering wheel. There was blood on his head and his clothes and the car was covered in blood. There was no sign of life. I ran to my landlord's house and called for him to send for the police.'

The first policeman on the scene was Detective Herbert Weise, of the *Mordkommission* – the Murder Squad. Detective Weise had been on call that weekend, but he was expecting it to be quiet. Saturday nights were usually busy for the uniformed police, with a bit of drunkenness, maybe some fighting and perhaps one or two drivers taking to the road with too much alcohol inside them. But Osnabrück was a law-abiding area, and murder was rare.

An ambulance arrived shortly after Detective Weise, and the body of Felix Reese was removed from his cab and taken to hospital. The nurse in the ambulance found 280DM in Felix's wallet, 13DM in his side pocket and 68DM in his purse, a total of 361DM, worth about £32 in 1966. No sooner had the ambulance pulled out of Albertstrasse than the first taxi arrived. An alert had gone out over the taxi radios that a driver had been attacked, and feelings among drivers were running so high that they all raced to the

scene of the murder. Within twenty minutes of the
first call to the police, there were thirty taxis crowding
the area. Some of them had even dumped their passengers halfway through a journey in order to be there.
All of them refused to work again that night.

State Attorney Walter Hunger was thirty-six at the
time, a young lawyer who had moved up the ladder
fast. It was compulsory under German law to call the
State Attorney to the scene of a murder. Hunger was
in bed with his wife when the phone rang, and he
dressed and drove the four miles from his home to
Albertstrasse. Because of the taxis he had to park a
few hundred yards away and walk.

'My first job was to calm down the other drivers.
Some of them were nearly hysterical,' says Walter
Hunger. 'Others organized themselves and drove
around the streets, hoping to find the attacker. I tried
to persuade them to go home, but none of them
wanted to. Then I went down to the hospital where
the body had been taken. I saw the death certificate
– it said heart and circulation failure. So I asked to
see the body, which was packed in ice. I immediately
saw where the bullet was lodged in the head, and I
got the death certificate changed. The doctor apologized for doing the first certificate in too much of a
hurry.'

Marlise Liekam recalls answering the telephone in
the bedroom of their flat at about quarter to two. It
was another taxi driver. 'He said, "Don't get too
upset – something terrible has happened." He said
there had been an attack, and that our cab was involved.'

Georg Liekam leaped out of bed, dressed and drove
to Albertstrasse. He saw the cab, covered in blood
and badly damaged where it was rammed against the
fence. But he was told that Felix was alive when he
was taken to hospital.

'I feared the worst because there was so much blood,' he says.

In the early hours of the morning Georg was taken to the hospital to identify the body.

'I felt so distressed, seeing Felix lying there. I knew I had to stay calm, but I felt like crying. He had been such a good man, and I knew his wife and daughter – he had brought them round to meet us. Felix was very popular with the other drivers – they all felt very distressed. And they also all knew that it could just as easily have been one of them.'

It was at six o'clock on Sunday morning that Georg and another driver went to Schinkel, to the road where Felix lived. Liesel Reese and her daughter Kirsten were asleep in bed.

'It was still dark when they knocked at my door,' says Liesel. 'At first I thought that Felix had forgotten his key, but then I noticed the time on the clock – he wasn't due to come home until about half-past seven.

'I went downstairs in my night clothes and let them in. I could tell from their faces that something was seriously wrong, but they said I should get dressed first. They sat in the living room in silence while I put my clothes on, and I guessed there had been an accident. I didn't think that Felix was dead. I don't remember what they said, or how they told me. I don't remember anything very much about that Sunday at all. I know I went downstairs and got my father, and he took care of all the things that needed doing. I was too shocked to take it in, and there were so many people around the house all day it was chaos. I didn't cry that first day – I was too numb. It all seemed unreal.'

By eight o'clock Liesel's home was besieged by newspaper reporters. Murders of taxi drivers were a very big story all over Germany, and reporters had got to the scene of the shooting as fast as the taxi drivers.

Liesel continues with the story: 'There was just no
time to sit Kirsten on my lap and tell her, but I was
frightened that she would go outside and hear it from
someone else. She knew that there was something
very important going on, and she was very upset – she
would leave the room as soon as anyone came in.'

Liesel was not taken to. see the body, which had
already been formally identified by Georg Liekam.
Today, Liesel regrets not seeing it.

'I think it would have helped me to come to terms
with Felix's death better. I did not accept it, not for a
long time. I kept expecting him to walk in. I kept
talking to him, carrying on as though he was there. It
was a great help having my parents downstairs – but in
a way, too, my father doing all the business side of
everything meant that I didn't really have to face up to
my husband's death.'

It was the next morning, Monday, before Liesel was
able to sit quietly with her daughter.

'I had no sleep, although I tried going to bed. But
the next day the reporters were gone, and I sat with
Kirsten and told her that her papa would not be
returning. I don't think she fully understood. She was
only five, and her idea of death was a bit like going to
sleep – you. wake up again. She didn't realize for a
long time that she would never see him again.'

Georg and the other taxi drivers were almost as
shocked and as upset as Liesel. At the site of the
murder they erected a marble slab with a flame on
top, and two drivers stood on duty there from the day
after the shooting until the funeral. The people of
Osnabrück made pilgrimages to the spot to put flowers
on the memorial. All the taxi drivers in the city had a
collection and raised 800DM (£72 in 1966 values)
which Liesel put away in a savings account in Kirsten's
name.

On Monday morning the death of Felix Reese

knocked every other story off the front page of the local papers. Henry Kissinger visiting Russia was relegated to the inside pages, as was the birth of actress Romy Schneider's baby. The gruesome details of the shooting were revealed, and there were appeals for information.

On the Tuesday the announcements column contained these two death notices: 'Our colleague, taxi driver Felix Reese, doing his job, was tragically torn from our ranks. Osnabrück Taxi Drivers.' . . . 'My dear husband, my good papa, our good son, son-in-law, brother, brother-in-law and uncle. Felix Reese tragically torn from us. He died in the bloom of his youth, at thirty.'

The police brought Felix's glasses and driving licence round to Liesel, and told her that she could have his clothes if she signed for them. But they warned her that they were covered in blood, so Liesel asked for them to be destroyed.

The money he had on him that night, his takings, were taken around to Georg Liekam's. The bundle of notes was left on a table, and the Liekams' dog, a poodle, leaped up and chewed at them.

'He never did anything like that before or afterwards,' says Marlise Liekam.

The cab that Felix had been driving, the black Mercedes, was impounded by the police for a week. When it was returned to Georg Liekam it was still caked with blood, and Georg had to ask around until he found a young man at his local garage who was willing to clean it. The cab was given a new taxi number and a new registration plate, because nobody wanted to travel in it. The old registration number was never reissued.

The funeral was held at 2 p.m. on Thursday, 8 December, at Schinkel cemetery. Marlise Liekam made arrangements for Kirsten, not yet of school age,

to be taken for the day to the kindergarten attended
by her own daughter. Kirsten did not understand why,
Marlise recalls: 'She cried a little because she did not
want to go, but the teacher looked after her well and
she was happy when she came home.'

The newspapers had predicted that there could be
as many as two thousand taxi drivers from all over
Germany at the funeral, but in fact there were only
three hundred. It was still enough to bring the whole
city to a standstill, however, as they progressed behind
the funeral cortege down Albertstrasse where the
murder had taken place, all flying black flags from
their aerials. The good spell of weather that the
country had been enjoying broke on that day, and it
rained hard from early morning until night, with the
rain turning to sleet at times. The scene around the
graveside in field 23C of the cemetery was a mass of
umbrellas. 'Like being under a roof,' Liesel Reese
says.

It was a very bleak Christmas for Liesel and
Kirsten. Liesel received a pension of 250DM (£22.50)
a month from the German equivalent of the Criminal
Injuries Compensation Board. Out of this she had to
pay rent to her parents, as well as electricity, gas and
water charges. She was left with 100DM (£9) a month
to live on. But it was not financial problems that were
the worst to begin with.

'I was still in a daze that Christmas. I couldn't think
straight. I was continually weeping, yet trying not to
cry in front of Kirsten. I couldn't really accept that he
wouldn't come back. I didn't want Christmas, with all
the jollity and celebrations. My parents were
wonderful – they did everything they could for Kirsten
and me. But I just wanted Felix.'

For Kirsten the Christmas of 1966, just three weeks
after her father's death, meant her last expensive
present: she was given a doll's pram and a doll, with

doll's clothes and bedding for the pram. Her father had bought it for her before his death, and hidden it away in her grandparents' flat downstairs.

CHAPTER 5

Court Martial and Trial

It was nine days after the killing of Felix Reese that Leslie Grantham was arrested. The German police had informed the British military police of the shooting the day after it happened, out of routine courtesy. There was no immediate reason to suspect a British soldier: although the type of gun used was identified quickly as a Walther .22 pistol, that was not a British army weapon and could just as easily have belonged to a German citizen.

'Our main reason for informing the British was because it was near Caprivi barracks,' says Waldemar Burghardt, who at the time was Deputy Chief Superintendent of Osnabrück CID and has since risen to the position of Chief of the CID for Lower Saxony. 'There was no clue that pointed us in the direction of the British, but it was a possibility we were always aware of. Osnabrück is the largest garrison town in Germany, and at that time we had ten thousand soldiers living here. I had six other murder cases on my books at the time, none of them involving British soldiers. But as a matter of routine we would keep the British military police informed. Co-operation between us was good and still is. Policemen are policemen – despite differences in language.

'Taxi driver murders were so common and caused so much publicity that we were hopeful we would get lots of information about the killer. We had already warned all drivers never to carry much money on them: we

suggested that every time they had more than 550DM
[£50] in takings they should hand it in at their office.
And after the Reese murder we recommended a
special protective glass between the driver and passenger, with a little drawer in which the passenger could
slide through the fare. Drivers used them for a while,
but as the epidemic of murders ended they started to
leave the glass open, and now we are back to cabs
without glass.'

The State Attorney's office put up a reward of
5000DM for information about the killing, and this
was increased to 8000DM by a publican, Herbert
Bremer, who ran the OAB Stübchen bar in Schinkel,
where Felix Reese often picked up fares. At the time
of the investigation Herr Bremer wished to remain
anonymous, and his identity was never printed in the
local papers. But there was a lot of publicity for the
reward on offer, worth about £720. A circular was
handed out by the police to all taxi drivers in the
town, asking for details of their movements on the
night of the murder – if they had seen Felix Reese's
cab at all that evening, if they had picked up any fares
in the same area of the town that the murder took
place.

One of the local papers, the *Osnabrücker Tageblatt*,
published an appeal in fractured English, as well as in
German, on the day of the funeral. Under the
headline 'We Must Find the Cruel Murderer' it said:

> On the second Sunday of Advent, thirty-year-
> old taxi driver Felix Reese was murdered. He
> died in the execution of his duty. Today he
> will be buried. His murderer, however, is still
> at liberty. We can all help that he may be
> caught and handed over to justice. Anybody
> who can give the slightest indication must
> come forward. This goes for the 143,000

Osnabrückers and also for the more than 10,000 Osnabrückers *pro tempore* – the British colony.

To this hour nobody knows where the murderer is hiding himself. Perhaps he is living in an Osnabrück family home. Perhaps he lives in one of the barracks of the NATO forces. Perhaps he is hiding in the open countryside. All can help to find him, German and British. The murderer has struck once. We cannot allow that another victim should fall into his hands. He knows he can only be punished once. His next victim may again be German, but it may be a British subject.

A sum of 8000DM is being offered for any clues that may lead to the capture of the murderer. This reward goes to whoever gives the police the right tip-off. The order and security of our streets are at stake – it is a matter of life and death.

The police had a description, given to them by the student who from an upstairs window had seen Grantham running away from the taxi after the shooting. They believed he was between five feet nine and five feet eleven tall – Leslie Grantham is six feet one inch. But the rest of the description was accurate: dark hair combed loosely back, age between twenty and thirty (Grantham was nineteen), and wearing a cloth overcoat of flecked pattern, similar to a pepper and salt tweed weave. The basic colour was light, possibly grey. The man's trousers and shoes were dark, and he wore no hat.

The day after the funeral the Murder Squad and the Osnabrück detachment of the Special Investigations Branch of the Royal Military Police issued a joint appeal for information in the *Osnabrücker Tageblatt*, again printed in English as well as German. A whole page of the newspaper was written in English, and an extra twelve thousand copies were printed and distributed free to the British barracks in the town. The headline said: 'The Murderer Can Be Caught. . . . But the Police Are Reliant on Everyone's Assistance.' It continued:

> Yesterday afternoon we, that is the people who live together in this town, no matter what their nationality, buried a fellow citizen, Felix Reese. Maybe the murderer stood at the grave too, right among us. So far there is no reason to suspect a stranger and it is therefore the duty of everyone to assist in finding him.
>
> The members of the Murder Squad are working feverishly to this end, but are not blessed with supernatural powers and must therefore rely on the steady and laborious piecing together of small and seemingly unimportant fragments of information which will inevitably lead us to the person responsible for the crime.
>
> Will you please make your contribution towards solving this crime? It is the duty of everyone and should not be left entirely to the police. We are not asking you to expose a petty thief or swindler, we are seeking a particularly cruel murderer in order to bring him to justice. Please help us to do this. A small and seemingly insignificant clue may be the key to success.

The newspaper appealed to taxi drivers to 'forget about old feuds and rivalries for the moment. Disregard for the moment the hard feelings involved in business competition. The response to a circular issued a

few days ago has been very sparse.' Another appeal
was aimed at guesthouse proprietors and their staff,
asking if any of their guests could have been the
wanted man. And then it listed ten specific points that
the Murder Commission and the military police
wanted answering, including information from anyone
who had seen a taxi on its way to Albertstrasse, or
who had seen someone with bloodstained clothing.
The police believed that the murderer might have got
into the cab at a bar, the Capri, in the town, and they
were appealing for anyone who had been there on the
night of the shooting to come forward.

'We didn't have many positive leads,' says
Waldemar Burghardt, of the German police. 'We
were trying to piece together any information we
could. But even though there was a good reward on
offer, the murder took place so late at night, with
nobody about, that there was not a lot of information
to collect.'

The Special Investigations Bureau of the Royal
Military Police were working hard. They toured all the
Osnabrück barracks, asking questions, searching
rooms and taking away for forensic examination any
clothing with suspect stains. At Belfast barracks – and
at Caprivi barracks, the one closest to the shooting –
all soldiers were fingerprinted, with an assurance that
the prints would be destroyed after the investigation
had been completed.

Rumours were flying thick and fast around Belfast
barracks. Fusilier John Moore was reported as a possible suspect, because on the night of the murder he
had arrived back with bloodstains on his clothes after
a fight with some German youths in the town. He was
quickly eliminated from the inquiry.

He heard the rumour that Leslie Grantham was the
killer – and ignored it. 'It didn't seem very likely. I
didn't think he was hard enough. And he was a model

soldier, not the type to do anything that would land him in trouble. I thought they were just rumours.'

The boxer who eventually went to the SIB about Grantham remembers that the whole barracks was buzzing about the murder – and enough people knew of Grantham's involvement for his name to be mentioned in the rumours.

'There were military police snuffling all over the barracks, mostly around his platoon. They talked to senior officers. Les was very cool, and no one said anything.'

When the arrest was made, less than two weeks before Christmas, a feeling of relief ran through the barracks. By now the whole battalion was buzzing with stories about Grantham.

'I didn't get any stick from anyone – he wasn't a popular guy,' says the boxer. 'One of the officers treated me a bit strangely, as though I was Judas Iscariot or something. But everyone else was OK about it. I was so badly shaken that I threw my next fight – I just couldn't get myself together. But I was able to sleep at night for the first time since the day he had told me about the killing.'

Back in England, the Grantham family heard of Les's arrest by telegram from the Home Office. Wally was at home when it arrived, because it coincided with the only strike that Boots' staff have ever had. Within twenty-four hours Wally, Anne and John had gone over to Germany. All their travel arrangements were made by the army. They went by ferry from Harwich, and were then picked up and flown to Osnabrück. When they arrived they were put up in a boarding house round the corner from the barracks where Les was being held under the guard of the Duke of Wellington's regiment.

'He seemed relieved to see us,' says John. 'Relieved that we weren't angry. Mum and dad were very normal, very calm and level-headed. I think that reassured Leslie.'

Angela Grantham heard the news of her brother's arrest from Graham, her fiancé.

'Mum rang Graham at work and told him to tell me. She was more worried about how I would take it than anyone else in the family. I believed it straightaway – if it had been John or Philip I would not have. I can remember feeling: "At last he's really done something terrible." I felt angry and I felt hurt for what he had done to the family. But I also felt very hurt for him, I thought he had just over-stepped the mark and it had gone disastrously wrong. At that stage I didn't think about the man who had been killed – just about Leslie.'

Philip, a schoolboy with O levels to take later that year, took the news hard, Angela remembers: 'He went very quiet and stayed on his own a lot. He always was a bit of a loner, but this seemed to make him more withdrawn. He had always got on well with Leslie: Philip worshipped both his older brothers.'

Wally Grantham's attitude to the killing exemplifies his feelings towards his son (and possibly also at this stage towards his other children). In the past, whenever angry fathers had knocked on the door demanding money owed to their sons by Leslie, Wally had defended his son but ultimately reached into his pocket and paid off the debt; now he took a similar attitude, totally believing Leslie's story that he did not know the gun was loaded.

Anne Grantham, on the other hand, was much more able to see the overall picture. She could not rid her mind of the image of the murdered man's family. She was worried for her son, but concerned for justice. In front of a senior officer she told Leslie that if it turned out that he had committed the murder in cold blood, he could expect no comfort or succour from her. The officer congratulated her on her words, looking as he did so at Wally, who was resolutely emphasizing his son's innocence. Sheer pride would never allow Wally to face up to the possibility that Leslie was guilty.

The family stayed for four days. John vividly remembers that his father, an ex-colour sergeant in the same regiment, was able to go into the sergeants' mess and buy a round of drinks very cheaply: 'Six doubles, six large splits, a packet of cigarettes and two bob change out of a pound.' They saw Leslie every day of their stay, but only for a couple of hours each day.

When they returned home, Wally flung himself wholeheartedly into organizing Leslie's defence. He employed on legal aid, the solicitors Kingsley Napley, a prestigious firm headed today by Sir David Napley.

Christmas that year was not easy for the Granthams. 'It was the quietest Christmas we'd ever spent. We all stayed home – I don't think mum went out once,' says Angela. 'We had the turkey and everything, but our hearts weren't in it. We sent cards and presents to Leslie.

'John started drinking heavily then. He'd always liked a drink, but he got to the stage where he could get through two bottles of vodka a day. He was drinking to forget what was going on.'

And if Christmas was bad, the New Year was even worse. In January both of Wally Grantham's parents died. Whether the shock of Leslie's arrest contributed to his grandparents' deaths we shall never know. His grandfather was seventy-six and his grandmother seventy-three, and both had been ill for some time.

Although they had been separated since he was young, Wally was in close touch with both of them. His mother still lived in Southwark: the break-up with her husband had come when his job as a tanner took him away from London, and she did not want to leave. She died of cancer in Guy's Hospital on 26 January. Four days later Leslie's grandfather Walter, who lived in

Chippenham, died in hospital in Bath. In both cases Wally Grantham was the nearest relative, and it fell to him to register the deaths and organize the funerals. John, the only member of the family with a driving licence, drove him down to Wiltshire for his father's funeral.

'He broke down in the car and cried like a baby,' John recalls. 'Perhaps he had been holding back his upset over Leslie, and that was part of it. But he was more upset than I have ever seen him before or since. It was a double blow, them dying so close to each other. I think he must have felt that everything was against him.'

For Leslie there was now a preliminary hearing, before the court martial, to decide if there was a case to answer. Although he was accused of a civil crime, the West German authorities had handed the case over to the British. There is an agreement between West Germany and the British and American authorities, just as there is with all NATO countries which have foreign soldiers based on their soil, that the crime should be tried under the laws of the criminal's own country.

Under the 1963 Status of Forces Agreement, the German courts could have claimed jurisdiction, but they did not. Walter Hunger, the Osnabrück State Attorney, wanted the case to be tried under German law because it was one of the few solved taxi driver murder cases. He wanted a big show trial, in a bid to curb the epidemic of murders, but he was over-ruled. However, because the murder of Felix Reese was such a big, newsworthy story the German authorities were more anxious than normal to clear it up satisfactorily, and they would have liked to have been more involved in the prosecution and trial.

Herr Hunger says, 'I wanted to include an interview with Grantham in my file on the case. But the British authorities would not allow me to. I went several times to the barracks to try and see him. They said I could not come in and he could not come out, so I suggested he be brought to the gate to speak to me. But they would not do it. They stuck to the rule book, even with such a big case.'

But the retired CID chief, Waldemar Burghardt, says the rule book was flaunted – the gun should have been produced by the British military police so that German forensic experts could examine it. 'It is perhaps a bureaucratic rule. After all, the gun would be examined by British experts before and after the case. But it is the rule, and it was broken. Otherwise, we were happy enough for the British to handle the matter.'

At the preliminary hearing, held in Belfast barracks just after Christmas, the boxer was the principal witness against Grantham.

'It was the first time I had seen him since his arrest. It was held in front of the Commanding Officer, and there were other senior officers there, in a large upstairs room in the barracks. Les was in handcuffs. He gave me a really hard, cold stare, and I can remember clearly that before the hearing started he was singing 'The Green Green Grass of Home' [the Tom Jones record that was top of the charts right through December and half of January]. I felt a bit frightened, but not of him so much as all the important people who were there. I tried to avoid his eyes, but he kept staring at me.'

The court martial was held at Bielefeld, thirty miles from Osnabrück, where all except the most trivial British military court martials are heard.

The court building there is modern, light and airy. But Leslie Grantham's first appearance there was not for his own court martial: he appeared as the principal witness in another case, while waiting for his own to come to trial. In admitting to the killing of Felix Reese,

Les had told the authorities about the bullying campaign that had forced his desperate need to steal. As a result, four men – Tony McDermott was one of them – had been arrested and were court martialled at Bielefeld in February 1967.

Nowadays army bullying allegations are commonplace, but twenty years ago very few soldiers dared complain they were being victimized – their complaints would have been taken as a sign of weakness, and they would consequently have suffered more at the hands of the bullies. But Les had nothing more to lose: he was facing a murder trial, so he told all about the branding incident with the hot iron. The ensuing court martial must have been one of the first examples of soldiers being tried for bullying.

Major Alan Westcob, a subaltern in the Duke of Wellington's regiment at the time and now retired from the army and living in America, tells how he attended the court martial and heard Les, still with the red scar above his eye, give evidence:

'Grantham told the court that he had been forced into the killing of the taxi driver by this gang. He had borrowed money from them and agreed to repay double the loan. When he could not pay, they threatened to carve up his mother on their return to the UK.

'To show him they meant business they laid a steam iron across the upper part of his face. The mark was clear for the court martial to see. Grantham told the court he was frightened both for his own safety and his mother's life. He said he was aware that the mothers of other serving soldiers had been threatened by the gang, and he understood that in at least one instance the threat had been carried out.'

The leader of the gang, McDermott, was found guilty of causing actual bodily harm, sentenced to two years and dismissed from the army.

'This man laughed out loud when he was sentenced,' says Major Westcob. 'Another fusilier got eighteen months and was dismissed from the service. The other two, regarded by the court martial as hangers-on, received detention sentences but were allowed to stay in the army.'

Major Westcob is convinced that the bullying was the only reason for Les to commit murder. 'He was a good soldier and would never have committed murder if he had not been so terrified of the gang. He acted under terrifying duress. Although there can be no doubt that Grantham killed a man, I believe there were extenuating circumstances. He was not a cold-blooded killer, but petrified and scared witless both for himself and his mother.'

Amazingly, these extenuating circumstances did not form a major part of Leslie's defence when his own court martial was heard in April 1967.

Wally, Anne and John Grantham travelled out to Germany again for the case, which lasted five days. John stayed for the first four days only, and then travelled home partly because he could not get more time off work, and partly to be with Philip and Angela. During the time that Leslie had been held in custody, his family had kept in touch with him by letter – and by occasional phone calls from his friends. He had even arranged for the soldiers who guarded him to phone his home with messages when they were off duty.

On two days of the court martial Liesel Reese was in court. In the small courtroom she was seated just a few feet from the Grantham family, and Anne was very upset to be so forcibly reminded of the reality of her son's crime.

'In other circumstances mum would have been the first to put her arm around someone who had been through such a tragedy,' says John. 'But obviously she couldn't. She was terribly upset, and couldn't even bear to look at the widow.'

Liesel, too, was distressed. She had not been informed of the court martial officially – indeed, she had only known about Leslie Grantham's arrest from the newspaper reports. She decided to attend the court martial for two reasons.

'I wanted to see the man who had killed my Felix. I wanted to know what such a man could look like. I had not seen the body of my husband, so the nearest I could come to convincing myself he was really dead was to see the man who killed him. And the other reason was to make a stand for all the other taxi murders. I wanted the court martial to get a lot of publicity, so that it would discourage people from killing taxi drivers.'

Liesel was accompanied by Georg Liekam and the man who had taken Felix's job: ironically, an Englishman called Charlie Wiltshire. Charlie, who was thirty at the time, had served in the Royal Army Service Corps in Osnabrück, then married a German girl and stayed out there after being demobbed. He had been driving a lorry long distance across Europe before he heard that Georg Liekam was looking for a driver.

'I knew Felix, but only to nod and say hello to. I had never had a conversation with him. Georg told me whose place I was taking, although obviously I knew – the killing was all over the papers. But I wanted a job that kept me at home more. And I wasn't superstitious about taking Felix's job, or even driving the car in which he was murdered. It takes a lot to frighten me.'

Another driver took Charlie, Georg and Liesel to the court martial in the same taxi in which Felix had died, and during the proceedings Charlie acted as interpreter for her.

'I looked at his parents, and I felt sad for them,' says Liesel. 'They looked so normal, and I could imagine a bit how they must be feeling. His brother looked so young, so good-looking, so very unhappy. But when I looked at *him* I just got an ice-cold feeling all over. He did not look at me. He ignored me. He seemed very cool and calm. I hated being there. I hated every minute. But I felt I was doing it for Felix, and I had to be brave. I did not understand what was happening, even with Charlie to help me.'

Charlie and Georg remember how upset Liesel was.

'She cried all the time on the way over there, which took us about three-quarters of an hour,' says Charlie. 'When I was interpreting for her in the court I don't think she really listened. She seemed very distracted. There was a lot of technical evidence about the gun, and it didn't seem very relevant somehow to her dead husband.'

'On one occasion the judge suggested she go outside,' says Georg. 'They wanted to look at Felix's skull, to see how the bullets had penetrated. But she insisted on staying.'

On another occasion the whole court went outside to look at the taxi in which the murder had taken place. Leslie Grantham, in handcuffs, was brought out to see it, but remained as impassive as he did throughout the rest of the proceedings.

The court martial – properly called a field general court martial – was heard by five officers, headed by Brigadier H. L. B. Salmon. The Judge Advocate General, Mr S. H. Bean (the senior officer from the Army Judge Advocate's department, which is the army legal department), was there to advise the officers on all legal points. The prosecution was led by Lieutenant Colonel Benjamin Odell, from the Army Legal Service, and Grantham was defended by a civilian barrister, Michael Eastham, QC, assisted by an officer from Grantham's own regiment.

Outside the courtroom each day were swarms of German reporters and photographers, and each newspaper covering the trial also needed its own interpreter. Leslie Grantham was charged under a cover-all section of military law that allows courts martial jurisdiction over civilian crimes: 'Committing a civil offence in that he did murder Felix Reese on 3 December 1966.' He appeared before the court wearing full uniform minus belt and cap: no soldier in custody is allowed these, partly as a signal of their disgrace, and partly because the belt could be used to harm themselves.

Over forty witnesses were heard during the trial, some of them forensic experts who gave evidence establishing that the gun found in the armoury was the one used in the crime. Walter Hunger, observing the trial officially for the German authorities, was surprised at how much time was spent on this evidence.

'Under German law, as the defendant admitted using that gun, we would have accepted that and not gone into forensic detail establishing what was already admitted. The German experts called – like the pathologist – found it very hard to comply with the rules of a British court. They were supposed just to answer the questions put to them. In a German court they stand up and tell everything they know. One expert, Dr Huber from Münster, an expert in gunshot wounds, got into hot water for refusing to stick to answering the questions. When he was told he must answer "yes" or "no" he said "No" – meaning he wouldn't answer like that. Everyone got very confused.'

Herr Hunger was also surprised about the informality in the courtroom before proceedings started each day, with the defendant and his family sipping cups of tea.

There was a dispute between the medical experts as to how close the gun had been to Felix Reese when it was fired. Grantham claimed that he was struggling with the taxi driver when the gun went off, but the evidence of one expert was that he must have been further back when he fired. But another expert supported Grantham's claim.

The student who had seen him running away and the nurse who had attended to Reese in hospital – and found his evening's takings still on him – gave evidence. So, too, did the other soldiers involved, including Michael Miles, who had been asked by Grantham to help him rob a German; the boxer who had helped hide the clothes and subsequently informed on Grantham; and Norman Marks, the armoury storesman who had supplied him with the gun and the ammunition.

The twelve soldiers who were called to give evidence travelled to the court martial by coach from Osnabrück each day. They all had to be present each day, despite the fact that some of them were in the witness box for only a few minutes, in case they were needed again. They spent the days in a waiting room, playing cards and reading newspapers. They were bored.

The boxer was in the witness box for a few hours. 'I was terrified. There were generals and a brigadier there. Les gave me a very cold, hard stare. When I was being cross-examined they tried to make out that I shouldn't have been frightened of Grantham, because I'm a boxer. But I'm only eight stone, and he's over six foot.'

It was Marks' evidence that was crucial. Grantham admitted killing Felix Reese, and he admitted using the gun supplied by Marks. All that was contentious – and critically so – was whether he had known the gun was loaded at the time he took it out with him on his mission to rob.

The legality of the situation, as explained to the court by the Judge Advocate General, was that if the court was satisfied that Grantham had known the pistol was loaded and intentionally pulled the trigger, he must be found guilty of murder. If he had known the gun was loaded and did not intend to shoot, he might be found guilty of manslaughter. If he had not known the gun was loaded, and therefore clearly had no intention of shooting, it was also manslaughter.

'As each day went on we felt that Norman Marks' evidence was being discredited, and we were confident that Leslie would get a manslaughter verdict and go to prison for five years,' says his brother John. 'We were really sure that everything was going our way. Leslie tried not to be too confident, but I think he felt it would definitely be manslaughter. When I returned home from Germany I said to mum and dad, "Don't worry, it's all going so well. There's nothing to worry about."'

But in his summing up for the prosecution Colonel Odell voiced the suspicions of everyone in the courtroom: how could an experienced soldier, who had himself worked in the armoury, not know that a gun was loaded? The defence summing up, by Michael Eastham, QC, stressed that only one person, Norman Marks, who until the crime had been Grantham's best friend, had given evidence that Grantham had taken ammunition as well as the pistol.

When, on the fifth day of the trial, 17 April 1967, just eleven days before his twentieth birthday, a verdict of guilty was given, Leslie Grantham betrayed no sign of shock or disappointment. His mother did: she collapsed in tears and had to be helped from the courtroom.

Before the sentence was announced, Wally Grantham went to the witness box to give evidence about his son's character. He told the court that he himself was a former soldier with the Royal Fusiliers, and that he had lost part of his right arm in the war. He said the family all got on well together and that Leslie had been a normal young man until he met his comrades in Osnabrück. He had changed after this, and seemed to think all the world was sworn against him. One of Grantham's senior officers also gave evidence that he was an exemplary soldier with every prospect of eventual promotion to the rank of sergeant.

After hearing this character evidence, sentence was passed. Leslie Michael Grantham was sentenced to life imprisonment, and dismissed from the service.

Ironically, had he been tried under German law, as a young man of under twenty-one the maximum sentence he could have received would have been ten years, of which he would probably have served only seven or eight. But under German law there would have been no possibility of the verdict being manslaughter, as anyone who kills during the commission of a robbery is guilty of murder. But the case would have been heard differently: there would have been less stress on proving his guilt (which he admitted) and more into his state of mind. Psychiatric reports would have been heard, and a thorough investigation into his family background presented to the court.

The German authorities were satisfied with the verdict. It made huge headlines all over Osnabrück, and was a major news item across the rest of West Germany. Although the local papers complained that several soldiers who had known the identity of the killer but had not betrayed him for nine days had not been punished ('With murder their should be no friendship, no loyalty'), by and large they were full of praise for the way the trial had been conducted.

Herr Hunger says, 'It was a very fair trial. A lot of trouble was taken to establish that Grantham was guilty. If he had not committed the crime, it would have come out. I was very impressed by the thoroughness of the trial.'

And the retired chief of CID, Waldemar Burghardt, says, 'As a professional policeman I am not responsible for a sentence. But my personal opinion is that it was a fair trial and the right verdict. If he had been found not guilty, then we would have worried.'

Liesel Reese also agrees with the verdict.

'It was fair. He was guilty. I thought that sending him to prison for life meant that he would stay there all his life. But I would not like to have seen him hanged: I do not think you avenge a life with a life.'

In fact, hanging had been abolished under British law only five months before Grantham was sentenced. Although the death penalty still existed under German law, it was imposed only for very rare and particularly serious crimes, and would never have applied to Grantham.

John Grantham heard the news of his brother's sentence while he was serving behind the bar of the Seven Stiles that evening. His parents had not had a chance to phone him.

'I travelled home overnight the night before the verdict,' John says, 'so I went to bed in the afternoon. Then I went to work at the pub, and a customer came into the off-licence and said it had been on the nine o'clock news. A few minutes later mum and dad rang me. They were both gutted. Mother was most upset. I think father is harder than her, better able to cope with these things. They had really believed he would get a manslaughter verdict, a sentence of five years – and after about two or three he would be out.'

John told Philip and Angela later that evening, when he got home. 'They both took it as well as could be expected. We all had to learn to accept it, but it took a long time.'

The next morning it made banner headlines in the *Daily Sketch*. But on the whole it was not big news in Britain, where there were plenty of other attention-grabbing stories. Fusiliers (from the Northumberland Regiment) were in the UN peace-keeping force in Aden and were being killed and injured in skirmishes there; Prime Minister Harold Wilson was battling against the unions with his ill-fated prices and incomes policy; Foreign Secretary George Brown was locked in conflict with General de Gaulle, who kept saying '*Non*' to British entry into the Common Market. So there was little room in the newspapers for stories about straight-forward murder trials featuring unknown young soldiers. The Charlie Richardson torture trial was running at the Old Bailey, fuelling the popular papers with all the gore they needed.

But in Orpington, of course, there was no avoiding the scandal. Angela offered to break off her en-gagement to Graham, to spare him any embarrass-ment. And John offered to resign from his job at the Seven Stiles. Both offers were turned down.

'Local people were very good. They were as shocked as we were,' says Angela. 'There was no bad feeling – everyone was very supportive. If there had been any-thing anyone could have done to help, they'd have done it. There wasn't. We just had to learn to live with it. It was all over the front page of the *Daily Sketch*, so there was no way it could ever have been kept secret.

'It hit mum really hard. She got home the next day, and you could see how badly shaken she was. I don't think she has ever recovered fully.'

CHAPTER 6

Life Inside

Leslie Grantham was flown back to Britain with an escort of two military policemen, and then taken by car to Wormwood Scrubs, where he served the first four years of his sentence.

The Scrubs is a large sprawl of Victorian buildings in west London, between Shepherds Bush and North Kensington, within sight of the busy A40(M) Westway. The street it stands on is called Du Cane Road, after Sir Edward Du Cane, who designed it in 1874 when it was built as a local prison. Sir Edward has gone down into penal history as a repressive and regressive influence. In 1865 he was the first chairman of the Board of Prison Commissioners, who administered all prisons, and under his guidance the Board opted for a punitive prison regime: 'Hard labour, hard fare and a hard bed' was the watchword.

By 1967, of course, these theories about the purpose and value of prison sentences had been long since over-turned, but the conditions in which prisoners were held remained Dickensian. The prison was no longer a local one. It had been built to hold 1024 prisoners, and is designated a Category B prison – for prisoners who need a high degree of security. With Wakefield and Gartree it is one of the main centres for life prisoners.

Leslie Grantham soon found himself a good role to play. He became the model prisoner – getting on well with the officers (but not well enough to be deemed a crawler) and with the other prisoners. Many of the officers were ex-army men. They liked Leslie's style and bearing – he still looked every inch the soldier. He was also determined to get his sentence over as soon as possible, so he did not get involved in trouble. Nor did he complain – another quality that endeared him to the prison staff.

He developed an ability to close his mind to anything other than the present; he did not dwell remorsefully on the past, nor did he waste time pining for the future. He perfected the survival technique needed by all long-term prisoners: one day at a time. So well did he master it that when an old school friend of his met him in the Scrubs eighteen months after Grantham arrived there, the friend commented, 'You would have thought he was just getting ready to go down to a disco, not facing years more of jail. He behaved like he was in there for three months, not life.'

Leslie adapted to his environment, and to some extent adapted the environment to suit him. He has always had, as his sister Angela says, tunnel vision about his own needs. He appeared to find it easy to get rid of the emotional baggage of guilt, either for his crime or the effect of his crime on his family, and single-mindedly get down to making the best of the circumstances.

And the circumstances were pretty grim. Twenty years ago Wormwood Scrubs was not overcrowded, but it was no four-star hotel. Like the rest of the prisoners, Leslie had to get used to using a bucket in his cell as a night-time lavatory, 'slopping out' or emptying it in the morning in smelly sluices. The food was of poor quality and the company could be very rough. Prison work was hard, and the pay of 3s (15p) a week scarcely fed his smoking habit. Like all prisoners, he quickly switched to buying tobacco and cigarette papers, splitting matches into four lengthways to make a box last four times as long.

Cockroaches are endemic in the Scrubs. On winter mornings, when the lights went on before daylight, the floors of the cells were seen to be covered in them. They would scuttle for cover in the light, and prisoners soon learned not to get out of bed in the dark unless they were prepared to feel the insects running over their feet.

Because of his ability to get on with the officers, Leslie soon enough found himself some of the best jobs. He had a cell in B wing, then the borstal wing for boys aged sixteen to eighteen who were waiting to be allocated to borstals or other prisons. Because they were so much younger than him, and because the population of the wing changed all the time, it was a relatively peaceful place. Giving him a cell there, because other wings were crowded, was a small example of the preferential treatment he managed to receive from the officers.

He also had a good job, dishing out food and handing out uniforms from the stores. The one made sure that he always got the best food on offer, the other that he had the best uniform possible. Like all the other prisoners he wore a prison issue blue striped shirt, grey trousers, black shoes and navy blue jacket. Whereas others had to make do with any approximate sizing that was issued to them, Les was able to make sure his was the best. And he kept it immaculate, soaping the creases of his trousers and sleeping with them under his mattress, as he had learned to do in the army. There was a barber in the prison, also serving a life sentence. He walked around carrying a canary in a cage. Before long, Les had persuaded him to cut his hair for him – there was no sign of it thinning then – and he used coconut oil to grease it.

He had regular visits every month from his mother and father. Sometimes his brother John would bring his girlfrend Anne, later to become his first wife. Angela and Philip would also visit. Wally sent in the £3 a month allowance that was permitted, so that Leslie could buy soap and shampoo. He also had girls visiting him – friends of John's, or friends of other prisoners who arranged it when they left. And because of his easy-going relationship with the officers, his half-hour visits often stretched to a couple of hours.

Jimmy Deighton, who had known Les at Herne's Rise Secondary Modern and at army cadets, joined him in the Scrubs towards the end of 1968. Jimmy was doing a six-month sentence for breaking and entering, and he served three months at Wormwood Scrubs before being transferred to a borstal.

'I met Les the second day I was in. He was serving on the hotplate. I helped myself to sugar and he told me I'd taken too much. He didn't recognize me but I knew him. I had heard he was in there. I was in borstal at the time of his sentence, but my mother had sent me a cutting from the local paper about it.

'After that meal he came to my cell, and had a bit of a set to with me about the sugar. Then he looked at the card on the door of the cell with my name on it. "Deighton? Where are you from?" he said. I told him and he started crying. I only saw him emotional twice – then, and when I left. He was so pleased to see someone from his old life.

'He had plenty of pull with the officers, and he got me a job with him and a cell opposite his. He enjoyed having a mucker. He had some friends in there, but no one he was close to.

'We worked on the hotplate together, dishing out the food. There was always plenty of aggro over food. People complain they aren't getting enough or they're getting the worst bits. Being two of us, we could set about them together. We didn't take any nonsense.

'It was a great job because we'd get up at 6.30 a.m. and there would just be three or four of us let out of our cells because we were the ones to work on the hotplate. That meant there was no trouble with slopping out. We didn't have to queue like the others did. And we had the lavatories and washrooms to ourselves. The hotplate was about twenty-five feet long and we'd stand behind it serving porridge, rolls, mugs of tea and sugar for breakfast. The other prisoners were unlocked one landing at a time, and then they'd take it back to their cells. It was the same at dinner time and supper time. We always got the best food – we had it first, while it was hot, and we chose the best chops and things.

'We had to wash the ground floor and toilets after breakfast, which was the worst part of the job. But even that meant we had more freedom than the others, and somehow Les always turned it into a lark.

'Then because we worked in the stores we weren't locked in in the evening when the others were. There might be new arrivals coming from the courts or other prisons who would need stores. If Les didn't like them he would give them all the worst, ill-fitting clothes and shoes.

'Sunday afternoons were a good time. The others would be locked in after Sunday dinner, but we would still be out to wash up in the kitchen. Then we'd go in the recreation room and put records on. He particularly liked "Captain of Your Ship". He'd fool around, singing to it. He always said at those times that when he got out he was going to be somebody. "One day I'll do something, show them all," he used to say. I always thought he meant he would be a pop singer. He looked the part – although his brother Johnny always looked more like a pop singer than he did.

'He could be quite tough, although he wasn't one of the really hard men. He wasn't particularly brave, but I think he felt better when he had a mate like me. Everyone was always a bit wary of the lifers who had committed murder. One night when the others were locked in we were playing ping-pong in the recreation area. Some of them, who resented us being out when they were locked in, could spit at us from the top landings. If their spy-hole covers had broken off they could spit through the hole, and it would come over the landing rail and down on to us. One guy did it and Les shouted to him, "I'll have you." When the cell doors were open the next morning we went up there and gave the bloke a right good seeing to.

'Where we came from we'd always had to be able to look after ourselves. And Les knew that the best way in prison is not to give in to anyone – don't let anyone get the upper hand.

'He had a great sense of humour, and that helped the time pass more quickly. He never liked queers – always made fun of them. On one particular occasion two of them came along for breakfast together, one of them with bright red dyed hair. I was handing out sausages and Les called to me not to let them have any. One of them asked why not, and Les said, "There's no way you're allowed to be locked in your cell with a sausage. You'll do things." Everyone else burst out laughing, but one of the queers slapped him.

'On one occasion he nearly got caught out going to chat up a really good-looking woman, who we thought was one of the official prison visitors. We were taking a tea trolley frm one wing to another, and there she was. The old Les charm started to work. But as we got up close we realized it was a bloke – one of the prisoners. Les laughed about it, but he was mad with himself. He hated queers and made no secret of it.

'He got on particularly well with one of the officers, a young guy in his twenties, who would bring baccy and sweets in for him. He used to share it with me.

'In all the time I was with him I only saw him down in the mouth on a couple of occasions, and then he snapped out of it very quickly. He seemed to be able to make himself snap out of it. There were other lifers around, but none of them seemed as well adapted as him. Some of them cracked up and had to be taken to the hospital. Others were very withdrawn and lived inside themselves.

'One, who had killed a secretary, was on the same wing as us when another mate of mine – someone Les knew slightly from back home – came in, just for three weeks. This mate was working in the toy shop when the lifer threw a hammer at him. It was a totally unprovoked attack, which damaged my mate's shoulder. When supper time came and the lifer's cell door was unlocked someone challenged him and threw hot tea over him – he was scalded badly enough to need to go to hospital, but Les and I reckoned it was justice.

'Emil Savundra was another prisoner there at the same time as us. He was doing eight years for a massive insurance swindle. He got out after six and a half because he had a bad heart. He wandered around unshaven, didn't care about himself or anything. That was typical of many of the better-educated prisoners – it was as though they just couldn't take it. Les wasn't like that. He kept himself immaculate. While everybody else had to shave in cold water, he shaved in the hot water he got for washing up.

'He quite liked his reputation as a hard man, but he was careful never to get into real trouble that might damage his chances of parole. But he didn't take any rubbish from anyone.

'On one occasion we were watching TV in the stores – God knows how he had wangled a set in there, but he had. He also had one in his cell, which nobody else did. It was one from the recreation area. Nobody complained about him having it. Anyway, while we were watching in the stores another prisoner came in and started getting a bit cheeky with Les. Les pinned him up against the wall and made his fingers into the shape of a gun which he put at the man's head and said, "Bang bang." Then he said, "If you don't watch it, I'll do you in."

'That was just to remind the other guy that he was a murderer, and afraid of no one. Anyone who has killed is a bit of a celebrity in jail because the others are all wary of them. Les quite liked that – he revelled in walking about, tall and straight, looking like a hard man. But he wasn't one of the really heavy ones. He was just like he was at school. He liked to be the big "I am."

'He talked a bit about the murder. He said he hadn't known the gun was loaded. And he was waiting for a date for an appeal. I don't think he was too hopeful about the appeal. He had taught himself to expect the worst. He liked talking about the old days – school and home and girls. He obviously missed women, but he certainly wasn't interested in the prison alternative: homosexuality. He talked about life outside in a very matter-of-fact way, as though he was going home next week. He had pictures of girls in his cell – mostly girls who had visited him or were writing to him. He had some of a girl called Caroline Burroughs, who had been in my class at school and was then working as a model. He had cut them out of newspapers. I didn't recognize her at first. But he didn't seem desperate about women. It was like everything else – he had it under control. I don't think I've ever met such a controlled man.

'When I left he was upset. We had got along really well, and I had hoped to do my whole six months there with him. But I got transferred out of the Scrubs. I only found out I was going the night before. I was upset, and so was he when I told him. He cried a bit, and hugged me to him. It was all quite emotional. And then he said, "Piss off out of here, I can't stand the sight of you no more."

'I wrote to him a couple of times after I'd left, but

The rebellious schoolboy; but the seventeen-year-old
Leslie Grantham was soon to conform to the ranks of
the Royal Fusiliers

Taxi number 46, registration number OS-Y-21 – the taxi that Lance Corporal Grantham took on the night of 3 December 1966, and where the body of Felix Reese was found (*photo:* Hartwig Fender)

'Are we sitting ducks? What happened to the death penalty for Taxi Murder?' Taxi drivers of Osnabrück demonstrate after Reese's murder (*photo:* Hartwig Fender)

Liesel Reese, Felix's widow, and her parents at the funeral of her husband. The day afterwards the headlines read, 'The murderer can be caught ...' (*photo:* Hartwig Fender)

Taxi drivers from all over West Germany formed a
convoy to mourn the death of one of their number
(*photo:* Hartwig Fender)

Thursday 8 December: the funeral of Felix Reese
(*photo:* Hartwig Fender)

In memoriam – Frau Reese holds a photograph of her dead husband (*photo:* Jens Bungies)

In 1967 the young Leslie Grantham marched to his court martial ...

Ley Hill open jail, 1976 – a snap taken by a fellow prisoner

Shortly after his release in 1978, Leslie Grantham poses in his sister Angela's back garden

A post-Christmas family snap: Leslie (foreground) with his father and brother John

The Grantham family. *From left:* Graham, Angela's husband, Walter, Jane, Leslie, brother John, Angela's daughter Claire. *Front:* Angela and son Alex

Philip Grantham – who died of the killer AIDS virus in 1986

Angela, Leslie's sister, who wishes she'd 'never bothered to go and see him' during his eleven-year prison ordeal – 'he's never shown any appreciation'

never heard from him. I didn't know at the time that ex-prisoners were not allowed to write to other prisoners.'

During these early years in prison, Les was pinning a lot of hope on winning an appeal against his sentence. His first application for leave to appeal was turned down. But his lawyers worked hard, and found another witness whose testimony they believed would have influenced the trial result. It would, they believed, have discredited Norman Marks' version of events and corroborated Leslie's. A second plea for appeal was rejected by the Courts Martial Appeal Court, on the grounds that convicted men have only one right of appeal. But after petitioning the Home Secretary, permission was given for the appeal and it was heard in October 1969.

A former soldier who had served with Leslie, Kenneth Nelson, gave evidence. But the appeal was dismissed on the grounds that his evidence did not directly touch on the vital questions of the trial: did Leslie Grantham know the gun was loaded, and did he have the intention of doing harm when he pointed it at the taxi driver. Both Leslie and his father, who had been banking on the success of the appeal, were acutely disappointed.

At the time when Jimmy Deighton was in prison with him, Les had not discovered drama. He had this vague, unsettling feeling that he wanted to do something with his life – 'show them' – when he left jail, but his ambition was unchannelled. Except that he knew, as he did when he was a child, that he enjoyed performing in front of others.

Quite what form that performing would take was revealed to him when a touring drama group came to the prison, and all the inmates went to the show.

Had Leslie Grantham ever seen a real live professional theatre performance before? Probably not.

There may have been compulsory school outings to a theatre, but on the whole, in the pre-comprehensive days when he was at school, theatre trips would have been the prerogative of the grammar schools. He had seen plenty of films, with all those childhood trips to 'the flicks', and he had watched plenty of television. But the Wormwood Scrubs show was probably his first introduction to live theatre, to actors as living, breathing, normal people only a footlight away from him.

At any rate, even if he had been exposed to theatre before, this was the first performance that he had actually seen and watched critically, not just as a part of the audience. It made him realize the potential of drama. He looked appreciatively at the skill involved in achieving what Coleridge described as 'the willing suspension of disbelief'. And he decided there and then, as he sat in the hall of Wormwood Scrubs with the rest of his life sentence stretching ahead of him, that he was going to be an actor.

He was so fired up by the revelation that after the performance he told those around him. Philip Meach, now an engineer, was in prison at the same time serving seven years for manslaughter, and he recalls Les's road-to-Damascus experience. 'He was transformed. That night he told us, "I am going to be an actor." We all laughed. Prisoners just don't become actors – not real ones.'

But Les was determined, and his first step was to join the Wormwood Scrubs theatre group. It was a surprise for the other members of the group: the theatre company was a meeting place for homosexuals and transsexuals, who enjoyed the chance to dress up and wear make-up.

Leslie says this about his introduction to drama: 'I was watching a prison play and said, "I could do that." Then some of the others turned to me and said, "Why don't you, then?" When the two guys leading the drama group went off to have electric shock treatment, I took over – it was as simple as that. I was the first non-poof to be in the group.'

The level of productions was not high. But they were popular, as they always are in prison. As Philip Meach says: 'Prison theatre is a cushy way of taking yourself out of the dreadful prison routine, the slopping out, the awful food and the hours of being banged up each day.'

Before Les joined the drama group, Philip Meach was not very impressed by him. Unlike Jimmy Deighton, he was not a close friend.

'I didn't like him. He'd murdered someone, but I never saw him show any remorse whatsoever. I never actually heard him boast about what he had done, but he seemed to revel in his reputation as a hard man. There's a strict class system in prison, and murderers who have done an out-of-the-ordinary killing are immediately among the elite. Grantham thought he was definitely Jack the Lad, and strutted about as though he owned the place.

'But the big boys were not impressed. Prison has some *really* hard men, but Grantham wasn't in their class.'

But the drama group gave Les no more need to seek friends or a role with the other prisoners. He found his niche. Philip Meach remembers the first production he took part in.

'It was a murder mystery, a kind of Agatha Christie thing with vicars, bodies in the parlour, a country house and a detective who unmasks the villain. Grantham got the part of the detective and he was brilliant. As much as I hated to admit it at the time, he was a natural actor. The rest of the cast were very amateurish, very self-conscious and always aware their cell-mates were watching. But Grantham was oblivious to everything except the part he was playing. He seemed to have swum into his element like a fish into water.

'He played the part deadpan, almost like an American detective, with that kind of clipped, corner-of-the-mouth delivery he has since used for Dirty Den. After that he appeared in every play they put on, and the prisoners cheered like mad. If there was a star of that nick, it was Leslie Grantham. He had a huge following, but with the exception of one or two female prison visitors there were no women fans.

'Even the prison officers used to looked forward to his next appearance. One screw told me: "It's a tragedy he's inside – he should be on telly."'

Perceptively, after Leslie became established as an actor – albeit only in prison productions – Philip Meach revised his original opinion of him.

'I began to wonder if he had been acting all his life. Was the tough-guy image and lack of remorse an act? Was acting his way of getting through all those years in prison? I don't think he knows where the real self finishes and the acting begins.'

Although they started from different positions – Jimmy Deighton as a friend and Philip Meach as one who did not like Les – their conclusions about him are remarkably similar. His ability to survive the rigours of prison life derived from cutting himself off, from treating it like a part he was playing. He already had an advanced appreciation of the value of acting a role in his own life before he discovered he could capitalize on his flair in a more structured way.

Soon, however, the new actor was to move to a new stage, away from the Scrubs. In 1970 the Home Office opened a new and experimental jail in Portsmouth – Kingston Prison. It was an old building, erected in 1877 as a local prison and used since the war as a recall centre for borstal trainees. It looks like a medieval fortress, with castellated towers, but its Victorian origins are betrayed by copious use of the arms of the Borough of Portsmouth decorating the stonework.

In 1969 it was renovated to take prisoners serving life sentences only, and all of them the sort of lifers who were deemed unlikely to offend again. They were men with no previous convictions – although this was later broadened to no previous convictions for violence. The Home Office explained the existence of the new prison by saying there was a need 'to provide a training ground for the less criminally minded prisoners: domestic murderers and those whose victims were in a relationship with them, and others'. None of the prisoners was regarded as needing medical attention. They were called 'domestic lifers', and came from prisons all over England and Wales, although principally from Wormwood Scrubs, Wakefield and Gartree. Kingston is unique, and has been acclaimed a great success.

The borstal buildings were converted and a workshop, library and more cells were built by prisoners from a nearby open prison. When the building was nearly complete a vanguard of ten lifers was moved in to decorate it. As soon as the work was finished the other prisoners, initially thirty of them, arrived.

After Wormwood Scrubs it was palatial. Every prisoner had his own cell; everyone was on first name terms, including the officers; and there were no trusties or redbands (prisoners with special privileges). All prisoners were deemed equal. Because of the small number of prisoners (even when full there were only 140 inmates) it had a friendly, almost intimate feeling about it. Although the prisoners were all Category B, which meant they had to wear handcuffs if they were taken outside the prison, the conditions inside were a mixture of Categories C and even D, as in an open prison.

There were no bars at the windows, although the windows were small and steel-framed. Each cell had a wardrobe, a bedside table, a bed, a chair and – a great luxury for prisoners – its own light switch, so that prisoners could choose for themselves when to switch their light on and off. They were allowed their own stereos and radios. The library was well stocked, and prisoners were allowed to have books sent in.

Instead of simply confining them for the terms of their sentence, Kingston was a brave attempt to root out the problems that had caused the original crimes, and to help the prisoners deal with them. A psychiatrist attended twice a week, and there were group therapy sessions every week. They were not compulsory, but in those days more than half the prisoners attended. Cynically, they knew that the games laid down by the authorities were the ones they would have to play if they wanted to speed up their release, and to be sent to Kingston was acknowledged as a first step in the right direction.

This showplace prison was on the Home Office map for distinguished visitors. The prisoners saw a constant stream of visiting psychologists and psychiatrists, parole boards, judges, probation officers, clergy and many foreign experts in penal matters. There was even a contingent of Russian judges.

But although it compared well with life in other prisons, it was still prison. All the prisoners were up at 6.30 a.m. to wash, shave and use the lavatories. Shared among every twenty-two to twenty-four men were three toilets, two urinals, one shower, seven washbasins and two slop sinks for slopping out. Because there was no overcrowding, and because the prisoners were hand-picked and the facilities new, it was possible to keep the lavatories and washroom spotless and clean-smelling – a major difference between Kingston and most prisons. The food was good, and again because of the small number of men there it was possible to serve it hot.

Tobacco, too, was relatively plentiful, as smuggling it in was easy. Prisoners and visitors used the same lavatories during visits, and tobacco could be left there by a visitor to be retrieved by a prisoner. Most of the prison officers, too, turned a blind eye to the smuggling but one zealous officer did report a prisoner to the governor for having tobacco brought in by a visitor. The governor was forced to fine the prisoner half an ounce of tobacco.

Leslie Grantham arrived at Kingston towards the end of 1971, a year after it opened and nearly five years after being sentenced. Like everyone else, he was soon immersed in the ethos of the place, exploring his reaction to stressful situations in group therapy and probing his past at his individual sessions with a psychiatrist.

The prison had a factory workshop, where in Leslie's time the prisoners were occupied soldering transistor boards. They worked regular hours there with a tea break in the morning and afternoon and an hour for lunch. There were education classes during the day (which allowed time off work) and in the evenings. Behaviour was good – there was never any trouble. One ex-prisoner describes Kingston as 'a gem of a place. So easy-going – no prisoner would spoil it, because he knew he might have to go back to one of the other prisons if he did.'

Even the officers were carefully chosen. Any who took the traditional adversarial stance with the prisoners and tried to promote aggro were soon removed. One officer was assigned to every four prisoners, and it was his job to get to know them well and anticipate their problems. Because of this high staff-to-inmates ratio, and because the prisoners were all long-term, it was possible for good counselling procedures to be developed.

'The whole emphasis was on finding out what made

you tick,' says Len Morrison, who was transferred to Kingston from Dartmoor. 'If you were in a bad mood nobody provoked you – they sat you down and asked you why. You got used to hearing all the details of other men's lives, things that men normally keep private from each other. Some of them told lies – they said what they thought the shrinks wanted to hear. But many of them at Kingston became very remorseful about their crimes, and it would all pour out. If you didn't have some great unhappy past, they tried to find one for you.

'I was in there for killing my wife's lover. I caught him in bed with her when she was pregnant. Simple as that. But the shrinks would try to link it with my childhood, my mother and father – every situation I'd ever been in.'

But even if some of the inmates were cynical about the effectiveness of the 'treatment' they were receiving, they were all happy to enjoy what went with it: a relaxed and easy prison life. Because most of them had served the bulk of their sentence by the time they were there (an average life sentence is eleven years, but some prisoners are released after eight or nine), they were anxiously waiting for 'dates'. A 'date' is the most prized possession of any long-term prisoner: it is the provisional date for his release. The whole purpose of Kingston was to rehabilitate and prepare prisoners for release, although most of them would still need some time in an open prison. A few were released straight from Kingston and as their 'date' approached, they were given more freedom. They were taken outside the prison, given money and expected to find their own way back.

After a lifer has served seven years, he is considered for parole each year. It becomes a private obsession, and when it is turned down prisoners can suffer serious mental problems. But at Kingston the staff were well aware of this, and a knockback was usually treated with a gentle chat and a cup of coffee.

'When you are serving a life sentence time stands still in your brain,' says Len. 'You think only of your life in prison, because if you start thinking of life outside it sends you mad. You can't live with a foot outside the gate – you have to make the best of life inside the gate. You watch TV and films but it's all unreal – you don't relate to it. It's a make-believe world in which you have no part. Les, like me, was well adapted to prison life. He took it one day at a time.'

Although prisoners were supposed to wear uniform, they could wear their own tee-shirts and trainers. And the overalls they were issued were cut down into trousers – and even tailored to give seventies' flares – by a couple of tailors among the inmates. Whereas in Wormwood Scrubs Les had been unusual in his attention to his clothes, at Kingston everyone cared how they looked. Shirts and trousers were always neatly pressed and nobody went around dirty.

Originally the prison had five wings, but they were later reduced to three, A, B, and D, with the remaining two being used for the gymnasium and administration blocks. Les was on D. In the early days there were so few prisoners that each wing contained only twenty men. There were television sets in three rooms, so there was no friction about which channel to watch (Channel Four did not exist then). There was a video, and films were available from the college film club, with very little restriction on the choice of material. Some were quite bloodthirsty, while others bordered on being blue movies.

The prison had a full-size snooker table, a gym and sports fields – used by the prisoners for sunbathing when the weather was good. Len Morrison ran the football team, a mixture of prisoners and officers who played local teams. He was always struggling to persuade enough prisoners to join, and on one occasion Leslie Grantham made up the team numbers. But Leslie has never enjoyed sport, despite being thin and fit.

'He bottled out when he came face to face with one of the other team in a hard confrontation. I don't think he's got much in the way of courage,' says Len. 'Physical things just weren't his scene. He was only happy on the football pitch when he was sunbathing.'

But the best facility of all for Leslie Grantham was the drama group. The prison had a stage in the dining room, and there were regular productions. Rehearsals were held in the classroom block. It was through his discovery of the power of words on stage that Les became interested in studying English as a subject, and it revolutionized his reading habits. The boy who had never from choice read anything more strenuous than the *Beano* or the *Dandy* was now rapidly working through the shelves of the prison library.

He dominated the drama group, although there were other good actors among the inmates. He enjoyed the acclaim it brought him, and although his following was not as big as in Wormwood Scrubs, he was soon the star prisoner again. He starred in a production of the farce *Charley's Aunt*, and in another play set in the First World War trenches. For the first time since he had discovered his flair for acting, Les was able to appear before mixed audiences. There were quite a few female staff working in the prison office block, and the audiences for the plays included officers' wives and female prison visitors, some of whom invited guests.

The presence of women around the jail was deliberate policy to help the lifers adjust to the normality of life outside prison. Les, young and good-looking, enjoyed chatting to the typists.

'I had to warn him off one of the young typists, because I thought he was getting a bit heavy with her. I worked in the administrative block, so I knew all the girls very well. I warned this particular girl to steer clear of him – partly for his sake as well, because it would have ended in disaster. He took the hint and stayed away,' says Len.

'He was very concerned about his image, even in there. We had a team of girls coming in to play badminton against us, and he wouldn't play because he was afraid he would be shown up by the better players.

'When he first arrived he used to play the hard man. But I believe he was acting a part. And he soon realized that wouldn't get him anywhere at Kingston, where the authorities weren't interested in hard men.

'Above all, he struck me as a survivor. A man who could adjust, whatever the circumstances.'

CHAPTER 7

Leslie Grantham – Actor

In 1976, the middle of the freewheeling seventies, Abba were dominating the charts with songs like 'Fernando' and 'Dancing Queen', and a new band called the Sex Pistols were doing their first gigs. That year, too, Leslie Grantham was transferred from Kingston to Ley Hill Prison, in the pretty Cotswold countryside of Gloucestershire.

Ley Hill is an open prison built on the site of an old US Air Force Hospital which specialized in the treatment of 'social diseases', less euphemistically known as sexually transmitted diseases or VD. It consists of twelve long, single-storey barrack buildings, still known as 'wards', each capable of housing between twenty-five and thirty prisoners. Some of the buildings are used for administration, one is a hospital, and the rest form accommodation for the prisoners. There are several newer, purpose-built buildings as well. Two of the accommodation blocks are split into separate rooms, while the rest are dormitories with a couple of single rooms. Those who are assigned their own rooms have their own keys.

Most prisoners arriving at Ley Hill are bowled over by the free and easy atmosphere and the comparative comfort, but for Leslie Grantham, arriving from the luxury of Kingston, it was in many ways a retrograde step. He was physically less well-off, sharing dormitory accommodation. Surrounded by three hundred other prisoners he did not feel the same sense of intimacy as at Kingston, although this was compensated by the freedom available, and by the certain knowledge that Ley Hill was only one step away from real freedom.

The majority of the inmates at Ley Hill in Leslie's time were long-term prisoners – lifers, or those guilty of non-violent crimes like fraud. But while he was there, prison policy changed – under pressure of chronic over-crowding in other prisons – and short-term local prisoners were brought in, which caused tensions. Short-term prisoners are not so jealous of their behaviour record, because remission is not so vital to them. And they tend not to regard the prison as their home, as the long-termers do, so they treat it and the staff differently.

It did improve the situation for the eighty lifers in one way, though. They were automatically awarded the privacy of their own rooms, instead of having to accept places in the dormitories. The rooms were approximately ten feet by twelve, with ceilings eight feet high. Prisoners were allowed to make them personal, with posters on the walls. Radios were allowed, which was a mixed blessing because the walls were thin and there was always a cacophony of competing stations. Although easy chairs were not allocated to each room, it was possible for most prisoners to get hold of one. Whenever a prisoner was being released there would be a scramble among the other long-termers and lifers to get hold of any useful possessions he might leave behind.

As in all prisons, there were trained tailors among the inmates who would adapt the regulation uniform. Collarless 'grandad' shirts were fashionable then, so they would remove the collars from the prison shirts. And when contrasting collars came in, they would turn collars round so that the stripes went a different way from the rest of the shirt. Les, as usual, was in the forefront of these fashion innovations. Leisure time was plentiful, and in the summer months all the prisoners were bronzed from sunbathing. Hair was worn fashionably long.

While he was there Les worked in the kitchens, and also in the prison officers' club. This job was deliberately allocated to prisoners being considered for release, because it gave them experience of handling money (decimalized since Leslie went to jail) and alcohol. It was possible for the prisoners in that job to get occasional drinks, but anyone taking too much would soon be in trouble.

The prison had the usual range of sporting activities, but the biggest plus for a prisoner like Les was the cultural life. Under a succession of enlightened governors, Ley Hill had developed good links with the community outside. There was a flourishing literature society and a debating society; while he was there an opera appreciation group was started; there were painting and ceramics classes; and gifted speakers came in from outside to lecture on their particular subjects. The girls from nearby Cheltenham Ladies' College even visited the prison to compete in debates with the prisoners. There were plenty of educational facilities, with prisoners studying for Open University degrees; Leslie himself took A level English. And while he was there a prison newspaper was started, which he became involved with.

Best of all, though, for Leslie Grantham was the drama group. It was run by a very talented and dedicated women called Madge Orgen, who lived not far from the prison. Miss Orgen is a personnel officer with a local company, but throughout her life she has dedicated any spare time she has to amateur dramatics, following in a family tradition established by her grandmother and continued by her mother. It was in 1970, she recalls, that she was invited by the then governor of Ley Hill, Alan Robertson, to run the dramatic society at the prison.

110

'I didn't want to. My reaction was to say no, I was very busy anyway and I didn't fancy the idea of doing plays with prisoners. But the governor was very persuasive, and I agreed to come and do one play. He told me that he was unhappy with the sort of plays the group had been producing, because he felt they were just an excuse for the prisoners to show off. He wanted a more serious approach to drama, and he wanted the plays to be all male roles, so that there were no opportunities for prisoners dressing up as women.

'He said he felt drama was an important part of the therapy available, but he wanted it better organized, with productions running to a timescale. He said he would see me again five days later and see how I was getting on – in fact he didn't talk to me again until we had put on three productions, and I was firmly involved. I think that was deliberate on his part: he didn't want to give me an excuse to pull out.'

The theatre was an old American army hut, with a deep but narrow stage which limited the types of plays the group could perform. Madge scrounged some theatre seats from a Gloucester drama group who were getting rid of them, and, together with the original seating, they made possible a capacity house of two hundred.

Normally, Madge teaches drama one evening a week at the prison. But when there is a production on she is there for rehearsals three or four evenings and all day Saturday. At first three or four productions were put on each year, with six weeks' rehearsals for each. Each production would have seven or eight performances in front of prisoners, staff and invited audiences from outside.

'There were only about three in the drama group when I joined, and they were very anti me. It took a while for them to accept me, and I had a terrible job recruiting enough new members to put on a play. I had to teach them lighting, props – everything. And they had to persuade others to come and work backstage, do prompt and help with costumes.

'I'm always working against their parole dates: I just get a production organized and one of my main parts gets released. But one bonus of prison drama is that you get a nice mix of accents. In a local amateur dramatic group you are up against the problem of everyone having the same accent.'

By the time Leslie Grantham arrived, Madge and her drama group were well established. She had expanded the repertoire beyond all-male casts, and had been given permission to bring actresses in to play the female roles. They were amateurs, too, most of them members of the local drama group to which Madge belongs. Musicals were also produced, but they depended on the musical talent available in the prison at the time, as Madge explains.

'Sometimes we've had a brilliant pianist to accompany us – real professional standard. Other times we've been struggling to find anyone who could even pick out a tune. So we've had to plan our productions accordingly.'

Leslie, too, had established himself as an actor at both Wormwood Scrubs and Kingston. So naturally within days of arriving he joined the Ley Hill Amateur Dramatic Society.

To start with, he and Madge battled. She recognized his talent right away, but was not impressed by his demands for starring roles. There were other good actors in the jail at the same time – one, she reckons, was just as good as Leslie.

'Besides, the discipline of taking smaller roles is important to an actor. None of them can expect always to be the star. I used to tell Leslie that if he was serious about acting after prison – and he told me almost straightaway that he intended going to drama school when he got out – then he must be prepared to take small roles.

'Sometimes he would sulk for weeks. He would leave the group and say he wasn't coming back. But we jogged along without him, and after two or three weeks he always drifted back. We had another battle, too, over a mannerism of his. He used his hands far too much when he acted – it looked unnatural. I never managed to wipe it out completely, because I don't think he believed me – he liked doing it, and he thought it made him look good. But since I've seen him acting on television it's gone. Drama school obviously wiped that out.

'He certainly isn't unique in his talent among prisoners. I have known several who had as much potential as Leslie, including the one who was in there at the same time as him. That one wasn't interested in going into drama after prison, though. But while they were there together they worked together very well. They were good foils for each other.

'Another ex-prisoner, not in at the same time as Leslie, is now at drama school. He's at least as talented as Leslie. He has a beautiful voice, although I suppose Leslie is a more flexible actor. Now that Leslie is a great success there is a tendency for a lot of prisoners to think they are going to emulate him, but of course most of them don't have the talent.'

As well as getting advice about his acting technique from Madge, Leslie Grantham also established another very good contact. A probation officer who knew him while he was at Ley Hill shared a flat in Bristol with a young actress called Louise Jameson, who was working at the Bristol Old Vic. A group of actresses went to Ley Hill to put on a revue, and afterwards the probation officer suggested that Louise and others could help the prisoners by visiting them. One of the actresses was forty-two-year-old Pamela Salem, who was introduced into *EastEnders* as the cool, sophisticated Joanna, the one woman who didn't succumb to Dirty Den's charms. Pamela visited several jails, but remembers Leslie particularly:

'I could see he had talent when I met him. He was very keen to act, but just a little lacking in confidence. I like to think I helped him to get over that and pursue his ambition.'

Louise, now thirty-six and most noted for her role as Bergerac's girlfriend in the long-running series about the Channel Islands cop, was in her mid-twenties at the time. She says: 'In Leslie's case we struck a good relationship from the start. I could sense he was an intelligent man who was interested in acting. He was naturally very frustrated in terms of being able to use the talents he had.

'I didn't know at first why he was in jail. In that situation you tell each other as much as you want to. He wasn't eager to discuss what happened. But I knew it must have been serious because he had been in Wormwood Scrubs previously, like a lot of lifers.

'I helped him, and took him through passages in plays. Through me he met a couple of other actors who also helped him. Then I saw him act with other inmates in a production of *My Three Angels*, and I knew he had something very special.

'Leslie's already paid a high price for what happened. He never tried to justify what he did and always said it had been a terrible mistake, one that he could never forgive himself for. Quite a few prisoners try to come up with an excuse for their behaviour and their crimes, but that wasn't him at all. He was suffering, and continues to suffer.'

Madge, too, did not at first know what Leslie was in prison for.

'I don't discuss it with them, and I never encourage them to tell me. I don't want to know. I knew he was a

lifer, that's all. For prisoners like Leslie, drama gives
their lives some structure. They discover they can make
people laugh or cry, or that they can tell them a story.

'Les got a very good grounding in a whole range of
drama. We read Shakespeare, although I don't think
we put on a Shakespeare production while he was in
there – you need too many actors. But we did Noël
Coward's *Nude with Violin*, we did *Arsenic and Old
Lace* and *Look After Lulu*, we did plays by Peter
Ustinov and Molière. Les was exceptionally good in
Conduct Unbecoming, despite the fact that he was in
one of his temperamental moods when we put that on
and threatened to drop out because he didn't get the
part he wanted. In the end he enjoyed the part,
especially as he had to wear a red waistcoat and black
jacket – Leslie was always very fussy about what he
wore. The leading lady was the wife of one of the
former governors of the prison.

'When Leslie did decide to accept a part, he was very
professional about doing it. He would take direction,
he would come up with good ideas. We all had a lot of
fun – he has a wicked sense of humour.'

With encouragement from Madge, Les started to
write drama as well as act in it. She gave him a
children's book called *The Scamp Family at Home*,
which he turned into a play for the youngsters from her
local amateur dramatic society to perform. He did it
very well, and was allowed out to come to the rehearsals.

He also wrote a play called *A Reason to Live*, which
was entered in the Gloucestershire Drama Festival and
won the award for the best original play. It is the story
of a woman in her forties, looking back over her life as
she waits for her lover, a soldier.

'It is searingly emotional in parts,' says Madge.
'Leslie told me, "There's a part of me in here, Madge."
When I said I would direct it for him I told him it had to

be my own interpretation – he wouldn't be allowed to intervene. He agreed to that and was very professional about it. Leslie chose not to act in it. We made the set all grey, like the main character's life, and we had picture frames on the walls of her room with no pictures in them.'

The production nearly did not make it to the drama festival, because of a strike by prison officers at Ley Hill. At the last minute they managed it, although the play had to be performed later than intended.

'Leslie was there in the audience to receive his award. We were all incredibly proud of him,' says Madge.

While Les was in Ley Hill there was a clampdown on the number of women allowed in to visit the prisoners, and to take part in the amateur dramatics. Madge was never aware of any ban on women coming in, but she noticed that those who did come in were scrutinized more closely, and their reason for being there checked more thoroughly.

T. Dan Smith, the former planning chief who was sentenced to six years for his part in the Poulson corruption affair, was in Ley Hill at the same time as Les – and he claims that the governor became suspicious of the numbers of actresses coming in to help the drama group prisoners.

'Les and I were good mates, but we had a real falling out over this. The governor and his staff want to help prisoners get out – they don't want to see them landing themselves in trouble. The actresses were coming in, and everyone was getting suspicious about what was going on – whether it was confined just to drama tuition. The governor told me it had to stop, and I tried to warn Les and the others off. The governor, the assistant governor and the welfare officer were doing their best to encourage the drama group, but they weren't daft. They knew that the girls weren't just coming in for drama reasons.

'I can't say exactly what did go on, because I wasn't involved. It was probably quite harmless, and I'm sure most of the girls and prisoners involved had the highest of motives, but it put everybody on the spot. I was so worried I remember telling my wife, Ada, all about it. I was afraid the whole pack of cards would collapse and innocent prisoners would end up losing remission. But in the end there was a clampdown and the visits were stopped. It was done indirectly – nobody was in trouble. Leslie was one of the governor's favourites, and he wouldn't have liked to have seen him in trouble. If a lifer gets 'sent back' – loses his date for release – he usually has to serve another four years.'

T. Dan Smith followed Leslie's drama career in Ley Hill closely, as theatre critic for the prison newspaper.

'There were others who were good, but he was exceptional. On the first night of *Conduct Unbecoming* he transfixed the audience. He had the ability to take everyone out of themselves, which is what prisoners need. They left their problems behind while they sat in that audience, and at the end of the evening he received a standing ovation. Playing before an audience of people who know you is much more difficult than playing to strangers, yet Les was always able to make us believe he was the character, not just Les playing a part. He took us over the wall and out of the prison. I have only ever seen one performance as good in my whole life, and that was by Thora Hird starring on television in an Alan Bennett play.

'I know that he was interested in drama before arriving at Ley Hill, but I hope he never underestimates the influence of Madge Orgen on him. She taught him all the discipline he would need in the real world of acting. She exacted a professional-type performance from all her actors.'

Mr Smith believes that Leslie's biggest problem at Ley Hill – and probably in the drama groups of the previous two prisons – was that he was associating most of the time with homosexuals and sex offenders.

'It really got to Les. He does not like homosexuals, and he certainly does not like sex offenders. But to take part in drama always meant working with them. They are the ones who make up the backbone of prison drama groups. It meant that Les had a hard time from some of the heavies, the hard-liners, who associated him with the company he was keeping. But Les was always firmly heterosexual, so it was unfair. It proves his dedication to drama that he was prepared to put up with all that for it – mixing with people like that made him tense.

'But gradually his reputation in the prison grew. He was sufficiently independent, a significant person. His stage reputation was genuinely appreciated by a high proportion of the men in there. And there were perks being in the drama group. They went outside to see other productions, and when their own plays were showing they had the chance afterwards to fraternize with the audience who came from outside the prison.'

As well as being lynchpin of the drama group, Les also became very involved with the prison newspaper and even edited it for a spell. He wrote an anonymous column full of gossip about prisoners and prison officers. Occasionally the paper was censored, but only rarely, and then usually because an article about politics was deemed to be inflammatory. Satire was very much in the air in the seventies, and under Les's editorship the paper moved away from straight reporting of prison news to a jokey, send-up approach. Criticism of the prison conditions, food and staff was tolerated, and so to some extent was criticism of Home Office policies.

It was this experience that persuaded Leslie, T. Dan Smith and an ex-solicitor who was also a prisoner to write and produce a satirical show centred around prison life. They worked quite hard on it, and even jokily got the solicitor to draw up a contract between the three of them stating that on their release any payment for work developed as a result of their collaboration would be split among them. The contract is invalid, as are all contracts between prisoners are.

The show consisted mainly of skits about prison life. Example: a prisoner goes to the welfare officer, crying, 'She's gone, she's gone,' and clutching a letter in his hand. The welfare officer, used to having to help men through the trauma of their wives leaving them while they are in prison, tries to calm the man down by giving him a cigarette. Every time he asks the prisoner a question, the man shakes and cries and has to be given another cigarette. Eventually the officer asks, 'When did your wife leave you?' 'Eighteen months ago,' comes the reply. But by then the prisoner has had six cigarettes – and anyone with any experience of prison knows what a precious commodity they are.

Ironically, not long after Les and his two co-writers had got most of their show written, the television series *Porridge* started. They watched it and agreed it was brilliant – and promptly ditched their own show.

'Ours was too similar to *Porridge*, but not as good. We abandoned it,' says T. Dan Smith.

Leslie was also a member of the Literature Society and the Debating Society at Ley Hill. Mr Smith remembers him speaking at debates.

'He used it as another platform to perform. He wasn't a logical debater – he didn't work out his arguments. He's not somebody who spends time preparing things – he rushes in and speaks without thinking through what he is saying. But he was fond of speaking, fond of performing. If a subject interested him, he would have plenty to say.

'In the literature meetings I can remember him becoming very animated when we discussed *Watership*

Down: he liked the book a lot, and wanted to talk about its significance. What he had to say was relevant. But on another occasion we were discussing the Russian writer Solzhenitsyn at quite a deep level, and Leslie just kept on talking, although he clearly did not appreciate the issues involved.

'His tendency to speak first and think afterwards didn't endear him to other prisoners in everyday situations. He was volatile, highly strung, like a racehorse. You knew that if you said the wrong thing to him he would fly off into a bad mood, and yet he would say very cutting things to other people. He is very witty, but often the humour at others' expense would be cruel.

'He was not one of the hard men of the jail. Compared to other prisons, Ley Hill has comparatively few hard men, but there are some. Les steered clear of trouble. Everyone at the end of their sentence is trying hard not to do anything that will give them a knockback. But he was tough, inwardly. You have to be to survive in prison, as I found out myself. If you aren't tough to start with, you learn to be – otherwise you sink.

'I survived by distancing myself from what was happening around me, and treating it as though I was studying it. Les distanced himself, too – you never felt you got really close to him. He would get depressed at times, but not too seriously. Compared to many of the others, he was very together.'

Madge Orgen, despite seeing him regularly all the time he was in Ley Hill, also feels that she never got to know Leslie Grantham.

'There was always a remoteness, a coldness in his eyes. He'd be talking to you and yet you'd feel he was actually somewhere else. I've seen it in other lifers. I think it's something they have to develop in order to survive. They daren't let go of their emotions – everything has to be tightly reined in. They seem to be reacting normally, but in their eyes you see this distance. I call them 'Ley Hill eyes'.

'Leslie still has them. I watch him on television and I can see that remote look, and I think to myself, "You may have come a long way, Leslie, but you still have 'Ley Hill eyes'."'

It was in 1978 that Leslie Grantham was released from prison – on licence for life. Prisoners who have served a life sentence are never really freed, and can be recalled at any time. For the first three or four years after their release they are under a supervising officer, who reports on their progress to C5 Division of the Home Office every six months. Their photograph and record are lodged at the nearest police station to their home, and they have to seek approval of their supervising officer if they wish to change addresses.

If, at any time after release, a lifer gets into trouble again, however trivial, he goes back under supervision again. And if the trouble is serious, he goes back to prison automatically. Every lifer, on leaving prison, is issued with a copy of his licence, under the Criminal Justice Act of 1967. The licence names the man and says:

1. He shall place himself under the supervision of whichever probation officer is nominated for this purpose from time to time.

2. He shall on release report to the probation officer and keep in touch according to the officer's instigation.

3. He shall receive visits from the officer where the licenceholder is living, if required.

4. He will inform the officer of any change in his address or job.

Every lifer has to sign to the effect that he has read and understands the licence, and he is supposed to carry it with him at all times until he is off supervision.

A condition of Leslie Grantham's release was that he would live for three months in a hostel attached to Wormwood Scrubs. While living there he worked as a painter and decorator – skills he had been taught at Ley Hill – with another ex-prisoner. There were still plenty of prisoners in Wormwood Scrubs who remember him from his celebrity as the star of the drama group. His good looks, his talent and his independence had made him a hero to many of them, and when the news reached them that he was living in the hostel prior to complete freedom, rumours went round the jail.

They centred on Les's success with women – an obviously sensitive and fascinating subject for cooped up and necessarily celibate prisoners. Les starred in the rumours as a rampant sex maniac with a list of beautiful girls queuing up to bed him. It was not a true picture of his life in the early years outside prison, but there was certainly a lot of time he had to make up for.

CHAPTER 8

Freedom – And Marriage

When Leslie Grantham walked out of the gates of Ley Hill he had been inside for nearly eleven years, and in that time the world had moved on. The currency had been decimalized in 1971. The number of cars on the roads had trebled. Inflation has soared through the roof. But there were some similarities between 1967 and 1978: another Labour government was in power, this time under Jim Callaghan. Flower power and hippies had been and gone, and with the release of the John Travolta film *Grease* there was a momentary fashion flashback to the fifties and early sixties, with sideburns, leather jackets and greased hair for the boys, and girls wearing stiffened petticoats and bobby socks – the rockers that Leslie had known in his teens.

Leslie travelled first to see his mother and father, who had now moved to Farnborough in Hampshire. He had £17.11 on him, the issued cost of his travel from the prison. John Grantham remembers his homecoming.

'It was a Wednesday. He refused to let any of us go to the prison to bring him home. He wanted to do it himself. He'd never been to mum and dad's house in Kingsleigh Road, so it must have seemed strange to him. I just wanted to hug him and give him a packet of fags and take him out for a drink. That's what we did in the end – we all went out for a drink to the pub down the road, the Fox. We've never been a family for celebrating at home.

'It didn't seem strange having him back. It was like

taking up where we left off. He looked very skinny. He was glad of the cigarettes. After all those years inside struggling to get enough smokes, it seems odd that he's now struggling to give it up.'

After his time at the hostel, Leslie, of course, had to have an officially approved address, but he did not want to live in Farnborough for two reasons. First, he did not want to go home to the kind of family nest that he had left when he joined the army. The world might have changed, but so had he: he wasn't the callow twenty-year-old who had started the life sentence. He was a well-read thirty-year-old, naïve still in some aspects of life, but with a better-developed sense of self and greater ambition than most young men of his age. The second reason was that Farnborough was too far from London, and Leslie was convinced that his immediate future lay at drama school.

So he asked his sister Angela and her policeman husband Graham McNab if he could live with them, in their police house in Bromley, which had the advantage of being near Sundridge Park station, only a short train ride away from central London. They were pleased to have him, although it was only a three-bedroomed house and they had to put their two children, then aged nine and seven, into the same bedroom. Angela and Graham had already helped by driving up to Ley Hill to collect his possessions. Graham did not ask for permission from his police bosses to allow his brother-in-law, a convicted murderer, to live in the police house with them.

'We took a risk,' says Angela. 'We didn't want to be told "No", so we didn't ask. Graham just told Leslie that he was welcome as long as he kept his nose clean. He travelled to us from the hostel by bus and train, even though we had offered to fetch him. He was shaking when he arrived, having travelled through heavy rush-hour traffic. It took him quite a while to get used to crossing roads again.

'He had some clothes when he came out of prison – jeans and sweaters and shirts, quite trendy. But he didn't have a suit. He had enough to get by. The kids were happy to have him around. He was a good uncle to them – he made time to kick a ball about with them or whatever.'

In prison Leslie had discussed with Madge Orgen and Louise Jameson how he should go about pursuing an acting career. He remained close to Louise for some months after his release. Later she said: 'What happened was between us and nobody else.' But he took her home to meet his family in Farnborough, and his brother John and sister Angela both believe that he was romantically involved with her. It was her influence most of all that persuaded him to pursue an acting career.

'A lot of people had told me that I should go into acting when I was released. But I wasn't sure whether they were just taking the mickey. It was Louise who finally convinced me to go to drama school,' explains Leslie.

Having decided to go, it was a matter of deciding which school and how to get in. With the approval of both his mentors, the Webber Douglas Academy was chosen. It was a school with a high reputation, it was in central London and it took mature students: it was a natural choice.

The academy had been set up in 1926 to train opera singers, but the emphasis shifted to acting when one of George Bernard Shaw's favourite actresses, Ellen O'Mally, introduced drama into the syllabus. The premises, in Clareville Street, South Kensington, include a theatre. Teaching at the school, according to the present Principal, Raphael Jago, concentrates on giving students a grounding in the demands of the classical stage. On this foundation is built a knowledge of the techniques used in film, television, radio and modern

125

drama. Singing, dancing and stage fighting are also taught.

The list of ex-pupils is impressive. It includes Donald Sinden, Michael Denison, Dulcie Gray, Penelope Keith, Terence Stamp, Samantha Eggar, Steven Berkoff, Charlotte Cornwell and Antony Sher. And now the name of Leslie Grantham was to be added to it, as well as Anita Dobson, his future co-star in *EastEnders*.

Leslie applied for – and got – a grant from the Borough of Bromley, where he was living with Angela and Graham. He had been saving the money he had earned as a painter and decorator, because he knew the local authority grant would barely cover the fees and his living costs. He enrolled for a two-year diploma course, the course the academy recommends for mature or overseas students.

He had to take an audition to get in. And although his educational qualifications fell short of the one A level and five O levels required, these were waived because he was a mature student. The academy was told of his prison background when they accepted him. Louise Jameson still figured prominently in his life, and he was seeing her regularly. Indeed she encouraged and coaxed him through his audition for the school.

Louise says: 'The big breakthrough for Leslie was getting into drama school. With his background it was a tough step. But once he was there he was on his way. His past was wiped out, at least temporarily.'

Two important women came into his life at the Webber Douglas Academy. The first, though – to be fair – not in order of importance, was Julia Smith, who would one day become the producer and overall supremo of *EastEnders*. Julia was a teacher at the Academy while Leslie was a student there, and although he didn't immediately impress her with his potential stardom, years later she remembered him.

The second woman was an Australian called Jane Mary Hickinbotham, later to become Mrs Leslie Grantham. She was twenty-two when she met Leslie, who was nine years older. Stunningly pretty, with blue eyes, fair hair and a slim figure, Jane, too, was doing the two-year diploma course at the Webber Douglas Academy. There she dropped the name Hickinbotham in favour of the stage name of Jane Laurie.

She was born on 21 August 1956 at Calvary Hospital, Adelaide, South Australia to Margaret and Alan Hickinbotham, and she has two sisters and two brothers. But there was no question of her parents having to struggle financially to bring up such a large family: Alan Hickinbotham is one of South Australia's major builders and developers. The family live in one of Adelaide's finest houses in the prestigious suburb of Unley Park, south of the city centre.

Her father took a science degree at Adelaide University, and took over the family firm two years before Jane was born and a year after his marriage. He is also a celebrated wine-grower, an expert in the culture of grapes and a wine merchant. In his youth he was a very good football player, playing for Geelong Grammar School (the school Prince Charles later attended) and for South Adelaide in the South Australian League. In 1947, when he was twenty-two, he was beaten by one vote for an award for the best and fairest player in the league. He was also a league football coach and a Melbourne district cricketer. During his National Service he was an air-gunner in the Royal Australian Air Force. In the late sixties and early seventies he tried to get into politics, but gave up after twice narrowly failing to be selected to stand.

His company has built over five thousand houses and developed thirty estates, of which five have been major, with more than three hundred houses on them. In the early eighties Alan Hickinbotham took on the challenge of building South Australia's first underground house, a revolutionary and luxurious all-brick structure built into a hill at his Clarendon wine property. On three levels, it has three bedrooms, a sauna, a spa and a smokehouse. Its temperature remains constant both summer and winter.

So Jane had a moneyed childhood, attending the best schools that Australia could offer. She says she had her first big romance – the only one before Leslie – when she was fourteen, with a boy from a similarly wealthy background.

'He was my only boyfriend in Australia. He owned vast tracts of property, and in Australia property owners are very, very rich. He used to drive cars into rivers for fun, and if they did not come out he'd go and buy another one the next day.'

Jane won one of only three coveted places awarded each term at the Sydney Drama School, but did not go because she found the system too cut-throat. She decided that if she was going to move away from home she would do it properly and travel to the other side of the world. She was serious about acting, and to Australians London was then the hub of world culture, the ideal place to launch an acting career.

'My first night in London I went to the university, rented a room and moved in with two Arabs,' she says.

But it wasn't long before her accommodation problems were solved. Her father bought her a house in Sydney Street, Chelsea. She was able to rent out rooms to other students – eight of them altogether – which gave her enough money to live on during her two-year course. She had entered Britain with a permit that enabled her to study, but she was not allowed to work in this country. As the other students supplemented their grants by taking on Saturday jobs, working in pubs at night, or even – if they were lucky – with occasional theatre jobs during their holidays, Jane

Leslie Grantham – now alias 'Dirty Den'

Mr and Mrs Grantham – Leslie and wife Jane Laurie

The other wife: with EastEnder Angie/Anita Dobson filming 'EastEnders' in Venice

Leslie and Susan Tully, who plays Michelle, before a charity run in East London's docklands

One aspect of life in the public eye: a well-protected
Leslie Grantham

Another aspect of public life: model Tracy Neve
plants one on Leslie (*photo:* Rod Pinchen)

Two rather more acceptable faces of fame: (*Above*)
Hands up for Dirty Den (*photo:* Picturepress),
(*Below*): A royal seal of approval for 'EastEnders'
stars from the Princess Royal

Twenty-two years on: Liesel Reese re-reads the papers
of 1966

The grave that no longer exists: Liesel Reese by her husband's tombstone (*photo:* Syndication International)

After protests from Grantham, Reese's skull is no longer an exhibit at a black museum of crimes committed by soldiers (*photo:* Brighton Evening Argus)

Murder of Herr Felix Reese – Taxi Driver

Herr Felix Reese, a West German taxi driver, was found dead in the front of his taxi at 0100 hrs on the 4 December 1966 in Albert Strasse, Osnabruck.

An examination of the deceased revealed that he had been shot in the head and the indications were that the weapon was probably a .22 Walther PP or PPK automatic pistol.

Enquiries carried out nearby revealed that a young man who had been seen beside the taxi had left the scene and headed towards an Army barracks. Further enquiries at Scarborough Barracks led to the arrest of 23982618 Lcpl Grantham I.M. Royal Fusiliers, who admitted borrowing a .22 sporting pistol from a unit armoury for the purpose of committing a robbery. He admitted responsibility for the death of the taxi driver and was subsequently charged and found guilty of murder.

Life goes on: future generations of Granthams continue to be the centre of press attention – Leslie and his son (Michael) are constantly photographed

wanted to be able to work. The easiest way for her to obtain permission was to become a British citizen, and the easiest way to do that was to marry one.

So in June 1979 Jane Mary Hickinbotham married Peregrine Tudor Llewellyn Lewis at Chelsea Register Office. Perry, who was also twenty-two, was a fellow-student and one of Jane's lodgers. His father, Peter, a retired publisher who lives near Hastings, insists it was solely a marriage of convenience, that his son was simply doing a favour for Jane and that, if Perry hadn't volunteered, she would have found another friend to do it. Mr and Mrs Lewis met Jane a few times, when they visited their son in London, and on one occasion he brought her down to their cottage. They found her a charming girl and a good friend to their son.

The marriage was annulled two and a half years later, two weeks before Jane and Leslie married. Tragically, Perry Lewis was drowned in the sea at Brighton in March 1985. Next to his clothes on the beach an empty half-bottle of vodka was found. The inquest recorded an open verdict. He had been working for the council in Bow, east London, at the time – a temporary job while he was still struggling to pursue an acting career. Ironically, his death occurred only a month after his fellow-student at Webber Douglas, Leslie Grantham, was launched to stardom in a new soap opera, *EastEnders*.

'We don't know whether he killed himself or not. Swimming in the sea in March is obviously dangerous. But we didn't know that he was depressed,' says his father. Jane attended the funeral, as did other friends from drama school days.

Perhaps to conceal details of this former marriage – which she has never publicly talked about – Jane Grantham has claimed that she was born in Bath and went to Australia when she was six, which would make her a British citizen and explain how she was able to work in London. When she was asked about her former marriage by a reporter all she said was, 'How did you find out about that? I've got nothing to say.'

It wasn't long after her marriage to Perry that she found the man she really wanted to marry: Leslie Grantham. They met when he was assigned to help with the lighting in a show that she and other students were putting on. Part of the Webber Douglas teaching method involves all students doing backstage work on others' productions.

He was older than the other students, more mature, more self-contained. The college buzzed with rumours about his previous life: to the girl students he was an exciting and dangerous creature. Jane promised her group of friends she would 'check him out', and walked across to start talking to him. The ultra-sensitive, ultra-self-conscious Leslie, not out of prison long enough to have gained any confidence in his skills with women, believed the gang of girls were taking the mickey out of him.

'I thought she was winding me up,' he says. I'm a very insecure person and I don't have a good opinion of myself. So when an attractive person talks to me like that, I think it's a wind-up.'

Jane says, 'We didn't like each other at first. But the chemistry must have been right. He was saying things like "Why not come out, baby, shake it up and razzmatazz." I was trying to be nice to him. But he had seen me coming over from the group of girls and thought I wasn't serious.'

When they did arrange dates, Jane reckons Leslie stood her up three times – again, still convinced that he was somehow the butt of a huge practical joke.

But Jane persisted, ignoring the humiliation of being publicly stood up when Leslie failed to meet her in a pub used by many of their fellow-students. Eventually they met in the street, but by this time Jane was determined to have nothing to do with him. Her resolution crumbled when he called her across to him.

'Once I was standing next to him I just went "Aaaah". I was absolutely useless, but you do behave oddly when you really love somebody. Then when we did finally go out together – first to dinner in the West End and on to a party – he met a girl who thought that *she* was supposed to be going out with him that night.'

While his romance with Jane was blossoming, Leslie was still supposed to be living with Angela and Graham. But he was never there and Graham, concerned for his police career, was worried. Whenever Angela reminded Leslie that the terms of his parole included living at their address, he told her that if anyone checked up on him she should say he had just popped out. Fortunately – as his popping out involved days on end – nobody did check, and he was released from his licence conditions quite quickly.

Angela and Graham would not see much more of Leslie – except when he and Jane were too broke to afford a Christmas lunch, when they would ring Angela before descending on her for Christmas Day.

'They arrived late and fairly drunk one year. We'd waited for them, so the meal was ruined. Leslie sat there saying what a terrible childhood he'd had, talking about all the beatings he had been given by dad. I had to remind him of the truth. He got away with a lot at home – I was the one who was always in trouble. Even Jane had to agree with me that he was exagerrating.

'The only other time Leslie bothered to keep in touch was if he had a parking fine. No matter how many times we told him that Graham couldn't do anything about his parking tickets for him, he always believed that a brother-in-law in the police ought to be able to sort it out for him.'

Leslie and Jane married on 29 December 1981. Leslie has said that it was all Jane's idea. She proposed to him by telling him that her parents were coming over, and that they would be pleased to be at the wedding ceremony. He says he replied, 'Yes, dear, whatever you want.'

But the arrangements cannot have been quite so informal, especially as Jane had to get her previous marriage annulled. They were married at Fulham register office, and afterwards went for a meal at the San Martino restaurant with Jane's parents and their friends.

Leslie's family – his mother and father, two brothers and sister – were not invited and were not told about the marriage until afterwards. Angela's daughter Claire, twelve years old at the time, was particularly upset, because when Leslie and Jane had announced that they would get married one day they had asked Claire to be one of their bridesmaids. It was her second let-down that year – a relative of her father's had made the same promise and not kept it.

At first Jane's wealthy parents were horrified at the idea of her marrying a convicted killer, nine years older than her, and not, at that time, with an established acting career. But Jane claims that when they met him he won them over. It is certainly true that they are now won over: they are regular visitors to Britain to see their daughter and her children. Every year they send a large Fortnum and Mason's hamper to the three-bedroom house in Eddiscombe Road, Fulham where the couple now live.

Angela, who is cynical about her brother's motives in everything he does, thought he was incapable of loving anyone other than himself.

She said, 'He is a terrible snob, despite the fact that he makes his living out of his working-class background. As soon as he met Jane's parents I think he decided that his family weren't good enough to go to the wedding, and that he had no further need of us.'

After leaving the Webber Douglas Academy, both Leslie and Jane managed to find a reasonable amount of work. When they could not find acting work, they took any casual jobs going. Jane worked as a waitress, while Leslie did more painting and decorating, served in a greengrocer's and in a posh men's clothes shop.

Jane has appeared in lots of television adverts, including Ford cars, TWA airlines, Twix chocolate bars and Four Seasons soups. Her fresh young face is ideal for advertising. She is chocolate-box pretty rather than threateningly attractive.

Leslie landed the part of the second lead in a BBC play, *Jake's End*. He was in a children's drama series, *Dramarama*, in which he played a barge man. In *Dr Who* he was the mechanic to the leading Dalek — following in the footsteps of his friend Louise Jameson, who had played Dr Who's sexy girl assistant Leyla. He also appeared in repertory at Coventry, playing the butler in *A Little Night Music*, and as the Irishman who is Lady Chatterley's lover before she meets the gamekeeper. Leslie fitted in well with the rest of the company, working hard, making everyone laugh with his usual hard, cynical humour, and organizing the company's social life by getting everyone down to the pub.

He was selected for Coventry's Belgrade Theatre by the theatre's assistant director, Simon Dunmore, who remembers the audition vividly.

'His sheer presence made me sit up. That happens very rarely. I asked him what he had done before and he told me he had been in prison. When you saw him on stage he was something special. He has a magic which is indefinable, but it is there.'

His most challenging role was in a BBC-2 play, *Knockback*, in which he played a prisoner — without telling anyone connected with it about his past. But his most prestigious was playing a drill sergeant in *Jewel in the Crown*, the highly acclaimed Granada TV serialization of the Raj quartet by Paul Scott. He had been keeping in touch with Madge Orgen – he had called in to see her once, and wrote her occasional letters, as well as sending Christmas cards. He wrote triumphantly, telling her he had landed the role in *Jewel*, but urging her, 'Don't blink or you'll miss me.' Madge recalls:

'He was very excited – I could tell from the letter. I don't believe he had ever thought he would do more than appear in repertory. When he left prison that was his highest ambition. He loved the stage and he wanted to be connected with it and work with it for the rest of his life. But he didn't expect to be a huge star with a lot of money from it.'

If that is true, Leslie had reckoned without Julia Smith. And *EastEnders*.

CHAPTER 9

'EastEnders' – Early Days

The BBC wanted a successful soap. It had needled for years that Granada's *Coronation Street* always topped the audience polls, and while the Beeb had originally tacitly deflected criticism by implying that soap operas were outside their Reithian remit, it was no longer a valid defence. They had long since come down from the mountainside and competed with ITV for viewing figures, buying up American soaps like *Dallas* and *Dynasty*. But they had failed to come up with a home-grown product that would knock the *Street* off its perch. Early attempts – *The Grove Family*, *The Newcomers*, *Compact*, *The Doctors* – had all enjoyed a healthy but never overwhelming success, and since 1971, when *The Doctors* ended, there had been no further attempts.

Julia Smith, a drama teacher by background, had been at the BBC for many years. She had worked on a sixties' soap, *The Newcomers*, as well as on long-running series like *Dr Finlay's Casebook* and *Dr Who*. A well-established director, Julia eventually became producer of the BBC's extremely popular hospital drama series, *Angels*. When *Angels* was turned from a once-a-week series to a twice-weekly serial she called on an old colleague of hers, Tony Holland, now forty-eight, to work as script editor. Tony had worked for years on *Z Cars*, as well as on a number of successful Thames TV series. For five years the two of them worked together on *Angels*, but the programme could

135

never truly be described as a soap because it only went out for seventeen weeks of the year. The BBC were keen to turn it into an all-year-round event, but it proved to be technically too difficult.

From *Angels* came *Distrist Nurse*, with Nerys Hughes cycling around a Welsh valley on her bicycle – again with Julia Smith and Tony Holland in charge. Julia and Tony were a good team. They got on together well, and even shared a flat in Cardiff while making *District Nurse*. They were also very experienced and able to turn programmes out fast, having started work in the days when drama was transmitted live. And of course they had been working well together on the nearest thing the Beeb had to a soap, *Angels*. So they were a natural choice when, in March 1983, the BBC decided that it was going to enter the fray and produce its own successful soap.

Ideas were commissioned, and pilot scripts were written. In the meantime the BBC had other problems: where would the new series be made? Eventually they bought the old ATV Studios at Elstree in Hertfordshire, where the *Muppets* shows had been made. It was deserted and desolate-looking, but there was plenty of room and making the new soap there meant that other BBC drama productions would not have to be pushed out of their studios.

Two potential settings for the new soap were short-listed: one was a shopping arcade, the other a caravan site. Both were rejected: the shopping arcade was technically too difficult, while the caravan site did not have enough potential storylines. Julia Smith and Tony Holland are both Londoners, and felt strongly they would like the new soap to have a London background. Jonathan Powell, recently appointed head of series and serials at the BBC, agreed with them. So Julia and Tony began exploring the old East End, to refresh their memories and see if too many changes had taken place which might have eliminated the old sense of comradeship. They hadn't: the old East End was still there, with street markets and terraced houses flourishing alongside the tower blocks.

On 1 February 1984 Julia, then fifty-six, and Tony were asked to produce a format for the new soap. They had only a few hours to put together a rough outline of the setting and flavour of the serial, so that on the following day the Controller of BBC-1 could decide whether to go ahead with it. They wrote:

> The bi-weekly is an on-going serial about the life of a community in the East End of London. Our area is the poorest borough in London, with the highest crime rate, the highest unemployment and the largest collection of deprived minority groups – yet through all this apparent hardness the dry, sharp 'cockney' shines through. . . .
>
> The specific location is a fairly run-down Victorian square, part council-owned, part private-owned, and the regular characters are the inhabitants of the square. . . . As well as one- and two-storey houses the square has a pub, a mini-supermarket, a launderette, a caff and – under the railway bridge – the tail-end of a lively street market. 'Trendies' may soon creep into the area but for now it is basically working-class. . . .
>
> The bi-weekly, then, is about relationships. Who's doing what, to whom and where will be the constant gossip of the square. The bi-weekly is about different types of households and different generations of people, from babies to teenagers, to adults and grandparents. It's a small community that lives a fairly closed life and has many things in

137

common. Elements of gossip, intrigue and
scandal are high on the list of everyday
happenings and events. . . .

The following day the format was presented – and
accepted. It took a mere thirty minutes for the Controller of BBC-1, Alan Hart, to agree to it: a record in an
organization where decisions frequently take months.
Although the name had not yet been agreed on, *East-
Enders* had come into existence.

The new soap was scheduled to be broadcast for the
first time the following January. That meant there were
only eight months to get the old Elstree Studios up and
running, because the shows would have to be taped
weeks before they went out. Everyone connected with
EastEnders realized straightaway that a very tough production schedule would be required to make two thirty-
minute programmes a week – it normally takes two
weeks to produce fifty minutes of television drama. But
it was possible. After all, other soaps were doing it.
And although shows like *Crossroads* consisted almost
entirely of interior shots and were rough at the edges,
others, like *Coronation Street* were well written, well
performed and well directed.

The original plan had been to shoot the outdoor
scenes for *EastEnders* in a real East End square, but
gradually it dawned on Julia Smith that this would be
too difficult. It would involve numerous technical problems, as well as taking up valuable time travelling between the studio and the location. After she and her
designer, Keith Harris, visited Elstree Studios they decided to build their own East End square on a patch of
scrubby ground that had previously been used as the
building site in *Auf Wiedersehen, Pet*.

The detail that went into getting the square right was
impressive. Thousands of photographs and sketches of
the real East End were studied, plans were drawn up,

stocks of tiles and railings and old doors and window frames were bought when genuine old buildings were being demolished. Meticulous plans of the shops, café, pub, launderette and railway bridge were drawn, and the site was planned so that a genuine tower block – in Borehamwood, Hertfordshire – would be in the background of many of the shots, adding an authentic feel to the set.

Problems were legion. The fact that both Julia Smith and Tony Holland were tied up with other programmes on a day-to-day basis did not help. The BBC working methods, imposed on them by the unions, would have meant as many as three different teams of technicians working on the same programme: it took the setting up of a whole new unit to solve that problem. All sorts of different departments were getting involved, but the most important area of all had not been tackled: no characters had been dreamed up.

To get away from the harassment of the numerous technical problems Julia and Tony flew to Lanzarote, beyond the reach of a telephone, and spent a fortnight creating the EastEnders, the people who have now become welcome guests in the sitting rooms of Britain. They had known from the outset that the central pillar of the series would be a family, a large extended family. They based it on Tony's own background – his mother came from a large family in Walthamstow – and even pinched quite a few of the names from the same source (Lou Beale was an aunt of his, while Peter Beale and his sister Pauline were cousins). Around this family they wove a network of other characters, changing and adapting them as they went along: punk Mary, Lofty, Dr Legg, Ethel, the Bengali shopkeepers Saeed and Naima, the Turkish Cypriot café owner Ali and his wife Sue (Ali was originally called Chris, until they realized that he should have a Muslim name), the West Indian Tony and his son Kelvin.

Tony and Julia had always known that the pub would be a central place where much of the intercourse between these different characters would occur. Yet they put off creating the pub family until the last. The original names they came up with for the publican and his wife and daughter were Jack, Pearl and Tracey Watts, but these were soon changed to Den, Angie and Sharon. Den was described as:

> . . . a smart dresser. He changes his shirt twice a day, his shoes sparkle. He runs a good pub. He's firm and fair with the staff. The cellars are well-organized and spotless. His 'masculinity' is the key to his character. It was called into question at an early stage of his marriage and he's defended it ever since. Some call him a ladies' man (because of his good looks), others a man's man. . . . He's a con man with the gift of the gab.

They decided at this early stage that Angie would drink too much, that Den would have a mistress, and that Sharon would be trapped between her warring parents. They knew, as soon as they dreamed up the characters, that the pub would be the centre of a lot of attention – not just because it is a convenient meeting place for other characters, but because of the constant tension between Den and Angie, the endemic shakiness of their marriage and the threat of Den's mistress turning up on Angie's territory. They even explored the plot far enough ahead to know that eventually Michelle Fowler would become pregnant, and Den would be the father of her child.

When they returned to England, they recruited a team of four writers and commissioned scripts. Work at Elstree was going ahead, and a recognizable square was being built. A theme tune was commissioned from

Simon May, who at his second attempt came up with the now-so-familiar *EastEnders* music. Albert Square came naturally as a name for the square, which obviously must have been built in the reign of Victoria and her consort Prince Albert, and so even more naturally it followed that the pub would be named after the queen herself. A couple of names that Tony and Julia had written down in a cemetery in the real East End – Luxford and Copley – became the name of the pub's brewery, and the beer was christened Churchill's. A mythical London borough, Walford, was dreamed up, and it was decided it would be E20. At this stage they still had to decide on a name for the serial.

Finding actors was not as easy as it sounds. Julia and Tony insisted that they wanted genuine East Enders to play the main parts. Agents and drama schools were alerted and auditions began, and before too long Bill Treacher (Arthur), Shirley Cheriton (Debs), Sandy Ratcliffe (Sue), Susan Tully (Michelle), Anna Wing (Lou), Leonard Fenton (Dr Legg) and Tom Watt (Lofty) had been recruited. Finding a Turkish Cypriot to play Ali, the West Indian-origin actors for the Carpenters and two Bengali-speaking actors for Naima and Saleem was harder.

Letitia Dean and Gretchen Franklin were both signed up, David Scarboro was chosen for the part of Mark, even though Julia and Tony realized he would be difficult to work with. He was a teenager who seemed to be going through every bit as much internal angst as the character they wanted him to play, and they were worried that he would be too typecast. Peter Dean, so much a genuine East Ender that he still helped out on the family market stall from time to time, was given the part of Pete Beale, and Gillian Taylforth was chosen as his wife Kathy, despite the fact that she was considerably younger than the original idea for Kathy.

Wendy Richard was a natural for the part of Pauline

141

Fowler – the only thing going against her was that she was already a household name, and the policy was not to choose 'stars'. But she wanted the part, was good in it and didn't mind that she wouldn't be looking glamorous. What's more, when she teamed up with Peter Dean they looked believable as twins.

There were two very important parts still not filled: Den and Angie Watts. It was not Julia Smith who remembered Leslie Grantham from her days teaching at the Webber Douglas Academy, but when his name was suggested by somebody else it rang a bell with her. She recalled then that he was a mature student at the drama school. But she had never seen him acting – he was a unknown quantity. He had been born in inner London, but brought up on the fringes – not quite the genuine East Ender they wanted. But near enough to get him an audition.

In *EastEnders: The Inside Story*, their book about the making of the series, Julia and Tony describe their first encounter with Leslie Grantham. The book, although written by them, refers to them in the third person:

> He came into the office. Just about everything he said was a 'gag' but, when you looked at his white knuckles and the sweat on his forehead, you realized this was just a device to cover extreme nervousness. Despite his nerves, he read [the audition piece] very well. Julia and Tony studied him. Den had to be an unknown. Well, he scored full marks in that department. He had to be 'starry'. They'd reserve judgment on that one. But he couldn't be so 'starry' that he wouldn't accept BBC fees. No problem there, either. But also Den had to have panache, charisma, electricity.
>
> Mr Grantham certainly had something, a

good sense of humour for starters. But, more than that, tensed up internal emotion of some sort that was only just being held in. There was something behind the eyes, too. Barely contained violence almost. . . . Better think about this one.

After Leslie had left, they discussed him. According to their book, Julia recognized his sex appeal but Tony was concerned that he ought to be bigger – publicans, he felt, ought to be big men. It took them a while to come round to the idea of accepting Leslie for the part; after they had seen him he began to grow on both of them. The marriage of Den Watts and his wife Angie was going to be a strong theme in the new soap, and they needed an actor who could convey a lot of inner turmoil without sitting down and talking about it. Leslie's 'tensed up internal emotion' was, they came to realize, just what they needed.

The first actress they cast as Angie was Jean Fennell, a very pretty genuine East Ender. They were worried from the beginning that she didn't have the strength for the character: although Angie was all-woman, she was also tough, gutsy and in some ways ruthless. But they took a chance on her, knowing that she would look good alongside Leslie Grantham.

Within days of Leslie being offered the part he phoned Julia Smith for a private meeting. He had realized from the beginning that this was no ordinary part that he was up for. Although he had been told that Den was not going to be one of the main characters (the Beales and the Fowlers were originally planned to be the central characters), and although he, like everyone else, recognized that the new soap might be a monumental failure, he also had to face up to the fact that it might be a great success. And even if it wasn't, there was bound to be a flurry of publicity about it: it was being launched as the Beeb's answer to *Coronation Street*, and popular newspapers were already speculating about it. He knew that his own history might be uncovered. Had he been more sophisticated in the ways of popular journalism he would have known that it was a racing certainty that his past would be exposed. But even viewing it as nothing more than a risk, he knew it was a risk he could not take on his own.

He told Julia Smith the full story, and offered her the chance to replace him. He said he had not mentioned it before because he had not thought he would get the job. Julia Smith did not withdraw the offer of the job. In the book she says: '. . . he had paid the full penalty for a mistake committed in his past, and it was a Christian duty to forgive'. The newly appointed *EastEnders* publicity officer was also told.

Had Julia Smith accepted his offer to withdraw from the part it would have made life easier for Leslie Grantham. But he wanted to play the part of Den: it interested and excited him, and he was enjoying the prospect of regular work. And because the BBC were prepared to stand by him, their decision superseded any second thoughts he might have had about whether he personally wanted to risk the exposure of his past. He had chosen a high-profile profession, so he could not back away from the sort of high-profile exposure that most jobbing actors would jump at.

'Anyone who chooses to be an actor knows that their private life ceases to be their own. If they become successful then they have to expect it all the more,' says Julia Smith. 'Sooner or later it was something that Leslie would have to face up to. I did not tell the other members of the cast of his past, because I purposely keep clear of talking or being involved in their private lives.

'But when Leslie's story came out there was nothing but total support for him from both the cast and the

BBC. I have never had any criticism for employing him, and I hope Leslie is fully aware of our feelings on the subject. Would I employ him again with prior knowledge of the fuss the story caused? Yes, I would. He is in his role only for his abilities as an actor. As a person, he is a gentleman, and I admire him for that.'

Shortly before *EastEnders* was due to go into production – episodes are recorded five weeks ahead of being broadcast – Jean Fennell was sacked and replaced by Anita Dobson. It came as a great shock to Jean, and a massive disappointment. She had got on well with Leslie Grantham and felt she was right for the part.

'Leslie has a terrific sense of humour. He cracks jokes all the time. He was a hard man to fathom, though. His funny moods would sometimes switch to very serious. And at times he was very distant and hard to get through to,' says Jean.

But Julia Smith had not been happy with Jean's interpretation of Angie. There was a tearful and distressing scene, but Julia would not relent. She did more than sack an actress that day: she demonstrated to the rest of the cast just how serious she was about making *EastEnders* the way she wanted it to be. It was a quality of toughness that she was looking for behind the frailty of Angie, and that was a quality she felt that Jean Fennell could not bring to the part. But after that day there was no doubt in anyone's mind that Julia herself had that quality of toughness.

Julia, a divorcee with no children, was always referred to by Tony Holland as 'the governor', as name that was quickly picked up by the actors, whom she referred to as 'the family'. She had trained as an actress herself at RADA, but quickly switched to teaching and production. She is only just over five feet tall, but makes up for her small stature with a large and powerful personality. When a journalist dubbed her the

Godmother soon after *EastEnders* started, the name stuck because it apparently summed up the overall control she places on her 'family'.

She won't let any of the actors change their lines or suggest the ways in which their characters should develop, sternly taking the view that they are jobbing actors with parts to play, not personalities projecting themselves on screen.

'I've worked as a director on previous soaps and I've seen actors take over characters. They get an incredible shallowness because the actor only knows the character from his limited experience of life. Even in life you can't know how you're going to behave in any situation. That's why we don't let actors see scripts more than a week in advance.'

Anita Dobson was the last-minute replacement for Jean. Julia Smith remembered Anita as another pupil at the Webber Douglas Academy, there at roughly the same time as Leslie Grantham. It wasn't a detailed memory: she would not have been surprised if Anita had turned out to be unsuitable. But something about the young actress had caught her imagination, and she wanted to see if Anita had developed into the kind of actress she was looking for – someone who could bring a brittle quality to Angie, someone who could fight like a tiger with her errant husband Den and yet retain an air of vulnerability. As soon as Julia and Tony heard Anita read the part, they knew they had found Angie Watts.

Anita and Leslie acted well together, and their off-camera relationship was reasonably good, if not close. Leslie's capacity to get on well with people and make the most of whatever circumstances he found himself in was invaluable in the early days of *EastEnders*. Unlike some of the others in the cast, he had no objection to travelling to Elstree every day. He coped well with the six-day working week that was imposed, and he never complained about the late finishes on at least two of those days.

His sense of humour, coupled with that of Peter Dean, broke a lot of ice and cooled a lot of over-heated moments. The twenty-four cast members were working very hard, and under extreme pressure. The BBC publicity machine was swinging into action. *EastEnders* was in every newspaper and was being trailed on the screen. Everyone involved in it knew that a lot was riding on it. The BBC had given them two regular slots plus an omnibus edition on Sunday afternoons: it was an unheard-of commitment to a soap, and an untried one at that. Production staff were naturally on edge; everyone was touchy and over-tired.

The launch was postponed from January to February 1985, to tie in with the launch of the new three-times-a-week *Wogan* show. Before it hit the screen, the biggest-ever publicity bash in the history of the BBC was mounted, so that before Tuesday, 19 February 1985 at 7 p.m., almost the entire nation was familiar with the theme tune, the title shots and even many of the characters.

It was Leslie Grantham's voice that was the first to be heard when the programme finally started. He was seen kicking down a door and walking into a dirty room. 'Stinks in 'ere', Britain heard him say.

EastEnders was on the air.

CHAPTER 10

The Private Life of a TV Star

The immediate reaction to the programme was enthusiastic. There were a few unfavourable comparisons with *Coronation Street*, naturally. But on the whole the popular press welcomed the new soap with open arms: not just because it was good, but also because it gave them a lot more cannon fodder.

Quite how much they did not realize until three days after the first transmission, when the front page of the *Sun* was emblazoned with the headline: '*EastEnder* Star is Killer'. The secret that Leslie had thought might just leak out had taken less than three days to be screamed out. The newspaper had been tipped off, inevitably, by an ex-prisoner who had been at Ley Hill with Grantham. A search through the newspaper library had produced reports of the trial nearly eighteen years earlier. When confronted, Leslie himself said nothing, except to point out that digging over his past would upset his parents – a plea for finer feelings towards them than he has himself shown in subsequent years.

But both his agent, Bryn Newton, and Julia Smith confirmed that the story was true. Julia said, 'As a very talented and experienced actor, we were happy to offer him the role. He has sought to make a new life.' Bryn Newton said, 'When I took him on he said he once killed a man. But he has paid his debt. He is one of the most gentle, caring personalities I have ever met.'

On the evening before the newspaper came out,

Leslie and his wife Jane stayed home and refused to answer the door of their Fulham house. Leslie rang his parents, and they in turn rang their other children, preparing them for the next morning. The *Sun* story inevitably kicked off a whole series of follow-up stories, and it was not long before the first reporter had tracked down the widow, Liesel Reese, in Germany.

The press camped outside Leslie's home. Decoy cars were provided by the BBC to lure them away, while Leslie was smuggled in and out of both his home and the Elstree studios. The rest of the cast supported him, although for them it had come as a complete bolt from the blue. But actors are a tolerant lot, and there was no criticism of him for his past. The present was what concerned all of them: they were already working to very tight deadlines producing the show, and to be permanently besieged by reporters and photographers did not help. But the publicity certainly was not hampering the audience ratings, and they all had to be grateful for that.

Leslie said later that he was relieved when it came out. He offered the BBC his resignation again, but they refused to accept it.

'I went to the BBC and said, "Get rid of me if you want to. I don't want to do anything that will affect the programme." I think they would have done if I hadn't been an asset to the show. It all had to come out some time, and in a way it was a relief when it did.'

Although there were some outraged demands for him to be sacked, the vast majority of the *EastEnders* audience, already hooked on the show, backed him.

According to newspaper reports, Leslie received only three nasty letters, and he remembered listening to a radio programme where researchers asked people if they felt he should stay in *EastEnders*. Ninety-eight per cent of them said: 'Leave Den alone.' Leslie said that when he was offered the part he realized his past might all come out, so he told them all about himself. 'But they said I had got the part on merit and ability, and since the news came out no one has pulled their children away from me in the street. All my friends knew.

'My wife Jane knew all about me when she married me. She was wonderful when the news came out. She is a very strong lady and she can cope. But I suppose underneath all that it hurt a lot. She is lovely and we are very close.'

He said that among the letters the BBC received at the time were some from prison staff who had known him during his eleven years in jail, letters that said 'nice things about me'.

Although it is probably true that Julia Smith and Michael Grade, Controller of BBC-1, stood by Leslie Grantham for the purest of motives, it cannot have escaped them that the resultant publicity would, temporarily at least, help the show's ratings. From the word go *EastEnders* did well (seventeen million viewers tuned in to the first episode) and it would not have held its place at the top of the viewing poll had it not been good. But lots of good programmes have a struggle initially convincing viewers to switch on to them. *EastEnders*, with its massive hype, had no such problems. The publicity about Leslie Grantham trawled it even more viewers.

Had he been cast as a Mr Clean character, the revelations about his early life might have had an adverse affect on the show. But because Den Watts was a complex, difficult, slightly shady character, someone who might have murky secrets in the background, the truth about the actor seemed to enhance the mesmeric qualities of the character. The audience, especially the women in it, loved him.

When, eight months after the launch, it was revealed that Den was the father of schoolgirl Michelle's unborn baby, viewing figures went through the roof, with an extra three million people glued to their sets – toppling *Coronation Street* from the number one spot in the ratings. The *Sun* christened him 'Dirty Den', a name that would stick for evermore. Although to a large extent he was playing himself – Leslie has described himself as coming from the NAN ('No Acting Necessary') school of drama – the part was giving him plenty of scope. Den was juggling a wife who accused him of impotence, a mistress with whom he was having a very sexy relationship, and a casual affair with Michelle which had resulted in her pregnancy – with only the two characters and the viewers in on the secret of the father's identity. On the sidelines he had an adopted daughter Sharon, whom he idolized. There was enough there for any actor to get his teeth into, and on top of all that Leslie even had to risk acting next to Roly, the huge poodle that was the pub dog (with whom he had a love-hate relationship off screen).

Leslie himself says he does not have a lot in common with Den. 'I wouldn't want to drink in his pub. And if I was a woman, I certainly wouldn't go to bed with him. I just don't get involved in the same sort of messes he does.' But he says he has a lot of sympathy for Den, and really regards him less as Dirty Den than as Victim Den. 'But it just doesn't ring as well, does it?'

The episode in which Michelle (played superbly by Susan Tully) revealed to Den that he was the father had the nation on the edge of their seats. 'I put my heart and soul into that scene,' says Leslie.

His wife Jane, who shares with him the secrets of the script, knew what was going to happen when she watched it, but none the less she says, 'It was a marvellous performance, absolutely fantastic. I knew what was going to happen but I was still gripped by it. Leslie's a smashing actor.'

He deflected praise, though, by turning it into a joke.

151

'If I had tears in my eyes it was because it had been raining. Or was it because it was cold? I know, it was because my pants were too tight. No! I know what it was. Just before that scene I saw my wage packet and realized how badly paid I am. That's why I cried.'

He professed to be puzzled about why he had become every girl's favourite pin-up, and why the BBC were being asked for more publicity pictures of him than of any other star.

'I'm just a normal working actor trying to make the most of the mediocre talent at my disposal. Nah – I'm not a heart-throb, for God's sake. I'm a forty-year-old (well, thirty-nine) guy who's ugly and going bald.'

But the fans were not easily put off. In a way that had never happened before, in the eyes of the viewers the characters began to be confused with the actors. Newspapers were writing stories about Dirty Den and the others as though they were real people, as though what happened on screen had a reality of its own. Leslie quickly became one of the most-recognized male faces in Britain, up with Prince Charles and ahead of Neil Kinnock. Eight hundred letters a week were pouring into the BBC from viewers. Journalists, desperate for yet another Dirty Den story, dreamed up bizzare angles, even claiming authoritatively that his secret mistress in the show was going to turn out to be a man.

The effect on Leslie's private life was devastating. He and Jane could no longer go shopping without being mobbed. Everything he did and said was monitored. Although he was not earning a huge salary from the BBC (the actors had been employed at standard BBC rates) he had soon discovered that there was a lot more to be made out of Dirty Den. The character was so popular that Leslie could have picked up thousands of pounds a week doing personal appearances had he had the time. Although Julia Smith had decreed that none of her stable of actors could appear privately as their

EastEnders characters, in Leslie's case the confusion of actor and character proved advantageous. For others, like Linda Davidson who played the punk girl Mary, the character was so far away from the reality that Linda could walk down the road unrecognized – an advantage in terms of her private life, a disadvantage in terms of picking up extra cash for personal appearances.

Leslie, money-motivated as ever, was prepared to give up what little spare time he had left after the gruelling schedule of making the programme to earn extra cash. Although he and Jane had been making a comfortable living before – both of them had had a reasonable amount of acting work, and when not acting had taken temporary jobs – this was Leslie's first taste of big money. Four years married to Jane, and mixing with her friends and family, had changed him inordinately. She had taught him to drive, and he drooled at the prospect of owning a good car. His instinctive taste for fine clothes was now being indulged with Piero Monzi suits and silk ties, he had become an expert on wine (Jane's father's influence), and his naturally healthy appetite had been channelled away from the doughnuts of his childhood to the best French cuisine.

They were the same sybaritic tastes as he had enjoyed in his early life, but honed and redirected under the gentle influence of Jane and the peer group he established himself with at drama school. And now, with the money rolling in for the first time ever, he could indulge them.

'I'm not a beer drinker,' he says. 'I must be the worst guy playing a publican on TV, because I'm not a pub person at all,' he adds, conveniently forgetting how he had earned shillings collecting glasses at the Seven Stiles, and had worked behind the bar there when he was technically too young even to have been inside the place.

When asked what he would be drinking over Christmas in 1985, only ten months after the programme was launched, he had to spell the names of the wines to the interviewer. He chose an expensive French wine called Pétrus, at £16 a bottle, to be preceded by an Italian Chardonnay and succeeded by Asti Spumante to wash down the Christmas pud, and rounded off with a sweet Australian Beerenauslese. In less than eight years he had travelled a long way from the gates of Ley Hill Prison.

When, a year after the show started, the BBC tried to limit the number of guest appearances the *EastEnders* stars put in, Leslie and his co-star Anita Dobson led the revolt. The show's bosses would have liked the stars to make only six or twelve appearances a year, as some of the show's stars were turning up late and tired for rehearsals. But Leslie, who has never allowed any extra work he does to interfere with the programme, and is in fairness renowned for being punctual, professional and on top of the script, won the right for all of them to make as many appearances as they wanted to. His own income was boosted from the early days of the show by £1000 every time he opened a supermarket or attended a nightclub. By the time he had been in the show a year, he and Jane were driving his 'n' hers BMWs, and spending their breaks in five-star hotels – and the money he was getting for each personal appearance had upped to £1500.

By the spring of 1986, Leslie's star was firmly fixed in the firmament. He was getting three times as much fan mail as any other EastEnder. A Gallup poll revealed he was the man most women would like to share a steamy shower with. When he turned up at bingo halls or nightclubs for personal appearances, he was mobbed. Girls asked him to sign his autograph in all sorts of unusual places, including the tops of their legs and across their boobs, and on average two thousand autographed photographs were handed out wherever he went. Vicars preached sermons about him, and the press decided he would be the next James Bond. His appearance engendered the sort of hysteria once reserved for pop groups. Up-market writers like Jilly Cooper were gushing about his sex appeal, 'He reminded me of a rescued dog, mostly of an alsatian. He has the same long face, the watchful acorn-brown eyes, the wolf-like grace, the unpredictability and the aggression hiding the intense vulnerability,' she wrote.

Leslie himself had some problems adjusting to his new superstar status. He had from the beginning performed the same role among the cast of *EastEnders* as he had in local repertory company: life and soul of the party, always ready with a quip and a joke, defusing potentially difficult situations with his humour. This made him the leading man of the cast in more ways than one. Not only had his role expanded to be the most vital in the soap, but backstage he had become indispensable to the smooth running of rehearsals. The latter he was prepared to cope with: the prison years had taught him the value of adaptability. But he was still insecure enough to be overawed by his own public success, alternately decrying it ('if a microphone gets in shot on *EastEnders* it gets fan mail') and giving way to megalomania, referring to the programme as 'my show' and name-dropping madly. By and large, in the early days, the rest of the cast accepted these temporary – if revealing – lapses. They were all in the same boat – actors and actresses grateful to have found themselves a place in a soap that looked as though it would run and run, and only too aware of the frailty of their tenure (Jean Fennell's departure was not forgotten).

Leslie perfected a downbeat way of fielding journalists' questions about his fame. When asked why he'd never appeared on the *Wogan* show he said Wogan had had Anita Dobson, Wendy Richard and even Ethel's little dog Willy. 'All three have got better legs and are better-looking than me, including the dog. So why should he want me?' He was genuinely perplexed by the degree of public interest, and at the same time determined to make the most of it in case the bubble should burst.

'I'm actually very shy and not cut out for this sort of thing,' he said about personal appearances. 'I'm always petrified no one is going to turn up. In Newcastle I lasted seventeen seconds before the women pounced. The bouncer had to yank me over the bar, shove my head under his arm and charge out like a rugby forward. It could make you big-headed. It hasn't in my case. I think it's a bit daft. I keep doing these personal appearances because the bubble could burst at any moment and I could be back on the streets again.'

But the counterpoint to this shyness and professed dislike of publicity was that on occasions he courted it. When Prince Andrew announced his engagement to Sarah Ferguson, Leslie actually sent them a congratulatory telegram, thanking them for keeping him off the front page – an act guaranteed to put him right back on the front page, and an early example of his schizophrenic attitude to press coverage.

By the first anniversary of the show, Jane Grantham was pregnant. She had suffered an early miscarriage the previous year, so she and Leslie delayed public announcement of her pregnancy until March.

'Both Jane and I longed for a baby,' said Leslie, 'but we felt our careers had to come first. We're both doing OK now, so it seemed a good time. I'm absolutely thrilled to bits.'

So were the newspapers. It promised them the next chapter in the Dirty Den saga. But before the birth of the baby came a more sensational chapter. The *Sun* unearthed in Germany a file kept by the Osnabrück police, dating back to the time of the murder. In it were statements made at that time by Leslie Grantham. The *Sun* published them – with an added statement from Leslie's lawyers to the effect that he had not co-operated in the production of the articles, no money had been paid to him and any quotations from him were taken from statements made at the time. He was unable to stop publication of the series of features, but he was furious about it, especially as the *Sun* had advertised it heavily on television.

It reawakened the original furore about his past – only this time, with the show so well established, even more column inches were devoted to it than before. The *Star* weighed in to defend him. The *Sun* carried out a poll of readers – and discovered that 60 per cent believed that he should have been hanged for the murder, while many more wanted him sacked from the TV show, and yet others believed he should be forced to pay compensation to the widow. Even Louise Jameson, whose previous connection with Leslie was revealed, received hate mail from members of the public. Michael Grade wrote an open letter defending him. And Julia Smith, who has always fought shy of giving interviews, said:

'I sometimes think, "Christ, what have I done to him and his family?" What has the show done? In a democracy, and a Christian society, if you sentence someone to jail and they serve their sentence, then they have wiped the slate clean. If Leslie had taken an ordinary job he would have inspired hundreds of ex-prisoners that it's possible to make a terrible mistake – which he is the first to admit – live it down and start again.'

Gretchen Franklin, the actress in her seventies who plays Ethel, spoke on behalf of the cast about their admiration for the way he rode the publicity.

'Leslie's a strange man. I don't know him all that well – I don't think any of us do. But he's a kind man. He'll still do anyone a good turn. He's never dragged his troubles in here, never let go. We've read stories that he's crumbling under the strain. If he is, he's very brave. He holds on to himself marvellously.'

Leslie himself was not crumbling – he was furious. The original exposure had been inevitable, and he had at that time been grateful to have a part that merited so much attention. But now, eighteen months on, he had begun to believe his own myth, however downbeat and jokey he managed to make his success sound when he was talking to reporters. Actors who worked with him were beginning to realize the truth behind the 'my show' slips. He really had begun to believe that the success of *EastEnders* was thanks to him. So when the publicity got bad again he retaliated by refusing to toe the BBC line.

When he, Anita Dobson and Jane How (who played his mistress Jan) flew out to film in Venice they found themselves besieged at Heathrow airport by photographers and reporters, ruining any chance of filming secretly, and blowing the storyline that Den would find himself in Italy with both the women in his life at the same time. But as Anita Dobson and Jane How shrugged and smiled at the cameras, Leslie's bad temper spilled over. He swore at journalists, shoved other passengers out of the way and jumped to the top of a queue. When one photographer tried to take a photograph without permission he swore and shouted, 'I don't care who you are. I say no to pictures, so don't do it.' Leslie was convinced – rightly – that the BBC publicity department had deliberately alerted the press, and he had the biggest row he has ever had with Julia Smith over it. Although he was under contract to the show until the following spring, there were serious doubts among showbusiness reporters about him staying.

The reporters who travelled to Venice with him were expecting the worst: a week of Leslie in foul mood, refusing to speak to them. When he called a group of them over to him in the sunshine of beautiful St Mark's Square they were expecting trouble. 'We thought he would be giving us an A1 bollocking about press intrusion – all his usual stuff,' one of them said.

Instead, he verbally laid into the BBC, accusing them of playing a trick on him by alerting the paparazzi, and warned that he would not co-operate if 'any more stunts are pulled'. Then he started pulling stunts of his own. Instead of spending his evenings at dinner with Julia Smith and the rest of the BBC contingent – and although she had no way of forcing her actors to stay in line, Julia had issued a three-line whip for them to dine with her – Leslie began a heavy programme of fraternizing with the enemy, the reporters, for whom he had previously not had a good thing to say (he once described the dog Roly as 'like a *Sun* reporter – hangs around all day and never does anything constructive').

He took three showbusiness writers from popular papers out to dinner to an expensive waterside restaurant, and paid for the meal himself – despite the fact that any one of them would have been able to claim expenses for entertaining him. The conversation was 'off the record', and they all agreed to observe that convention. He relaxed, unwound and chatted freely. His street-sharp wit meant that he blended well with journalists, sharing the same sort of cynical humour. They found him congenial company, although his by now well-developed persecution complex showed, even if he had realigned its course. He voiced the opinion that Julia Smith and the BBC moguls were no longer the nice people who had stood behind him when his past was exposed. He believed that they had positively used his murder conviction to seek publicity.

His paranoia about the press proved to be, in part at least, justified, because in the succeeding two years one of the three journalists present has written about most of the topics covered at that dinner, causing problems for Leslie with other members of the cast. The conversation included his dislike of Peter Dean (Pete Beale) – mainly, he alleged, because Dean was persecuting Gillian Taylforth (who plays Kathy Beale, Pete's wife) with sexual advances, an allegation that has since been corroborated by Gillian Taylforth and denied by Peter Dean (who admits the mutual antipathy between him and Leslie, and says that it even ended up with them rolling around the studio floor in temper).

Leslie also made a joking reference to not fancying Anita Dobson, implying that she wasn't fastidious in her personal habits. This was later reported as him saying that she smelled, and caused an almighty uproar between the two of them, which Leslie wriggled out of by claiming that he had never said it and had been totally misquoted.

Another joking remark was that he was a virgin when he met Jane. He didn't intend the reporters to take it seriously and they didn't, until two years later when it appeared in print. Nobody who knows him took the claim seriously – although had he claimed he had never had a serious relationship before Jane he might have been nearer the truth.

Later in the week of filming in Venice, Leslie went out with the reporters again, only this time with all of them and with the photographers. He was more guarded in his comments, but was again using them as part of his war of attrition against Julia Smith. For the whole of that week his relationship with her was non-existent, and although it later became a good working relationship again, he has never reverted to his original glowing opinion of her.

On 30 September 1986 Michael Leslie Grantham was born at the Portland Hospital, a sturdy eight pound five ounce baby. During the pregnancy Leslie had given false leads about where Jane would be having the baby, changing the hospital three times in order to throw reporters off the scent. He claimed that some journalists were trying to bribe nurses to the tune of £500 to get pictures of his firstborn, but by this time paranoia about the press had well and truly set in. Leslie was travelling everywhere with minders – a couple of burly gentlemen who could shoulder his way through fans for him – and one of these was assigned to stay with Jane at the hospital.

Leslie was present at the birth.

'I didn't originally want to, but that's the way they do it these days, and I'm glad I did. It was the proudest moment I've ever experienced. Jane and the boy are in perfect health and we have never been closer as a couple. I'm looking forward very much to being a father and all that goes with it. It's going to be a very good time for us as a family.'

Although they were still living in the same house that they had bought for £70,000, with a mortgage, after their wedding, the place had been renovated and an extension added, and a nursery was ready for the baby. Because of a tuft of hair that stuck up on the top of his head he was nicknamed Spike. Leslie is a devoted father: the cast of *EastEnders* have even accused him of being a baby bore, producing pictures of Spike at every opportunity. Whereas he doesn't talk about Jane much, he never stops talking about his son. Before the baby was born he made it clear that it was a son he wanted, and he admitted he will spoil him.

The day before baby Michael was born, Leslie crashed his £14,000 BMW when he was hit broadside-on by a van on his way to Elstree. The car was a write-off. The day after the birth, he bought yet another car for Jane: a brand-new £12,000 BMW. Money was no problem, because even though his BBC salary was only £26,000 a year, he was upping this to over £200,000 with personal appearances.

The Leslie Grantham Story

The car crash is a good example of his schizophrenic relationship with the press. One of the reporters who had been close to him in Venice approached him to ask about the car and was rudely avoided: the subject was innocuous, the attitude inexplicable. 'You never know when you approach Leslie whether he will put his arm round you like a long lost brother or be totally rude and unco-operative,' says the reporter.

Soon after the birth of Michael the news of Leslie's brother Philip's death from Aids broke, and this created another storm of publicity. And Leslie walked straight into more controversy by turning down the chance to meet the Queen Mum and Fergie at the Royal Variety Performance, which was attended by twenty-six members of the *EastEnders* cast. Leslie was having a week's holiday, spending it at home with his wife and baby, and on the night of the show they were entertaining friends. If the Royals were upset, they didn't show it. A few months later he turned down the chance to meet Princess Di at a charity event – instead he was earning a fee appearing at the opening of a nightclub.

Rumours were growing that publicity pressures would force him to quit. His agent, Bryn Newton, admitted that Leslie was 'tired and edgy' – and offered this as an excuse for him seemingly attempting to run down a photographer with his car in a fit of temper. Ironically, that incident happened in the same week that he and Anita Dobson were handed the accolade of switching on London's Oxford Street Christmas lights. On occasions like that he was still able to smile obligingly for the fans, but increasingly the cheerful, jokey exterior of the early days of *EastEnders* was gone, and was replaced by unremitting bad temper.

In one savage outburst he told the rest of the cast exactly what he thought of them – and of himself. He is alleged to have said, 'Without me there would be no show. This whole series revolves around me. If I leave the show it will go down the pan. You lot are all idiots.'

On another occasion, when he tripped on the flimsy stairs at the Queen Vic and the set around him collapsed, he screamed, 'I could have broken my neck – and then where would this —ing show be?'

He wasn't the only one suffering from the pressures of such a demanding work routine. Other members of the cast came and went, some of them – like Ross Davidson and Shirley Cheriton – amid rumour and speculation of off-screen rows and scandal. In the spring of 1987 even Julia Smith succumbed: Tony Virgo was appointed producer of the show, working under her in her new role as executive producer. But it was still too much of her baby for her to let go completely, and she remained very much in control.

In fact, the tight control she exerted over her 'family' is the cause of many of the problems. When he left, Ross Davidson accused her of treating her actors like babies. They have to have her permission for every personal appearance, every interview they give, every charity event they appear at; and they are forbidden to travel more than fifty miles outside London on weekdays. When the cast attended the Royal Variety Peformance they were bussed there, with minders to look after them, and told who they were allowed to speak to – which is probably the real reason that Leslie Grantham refused to attend, coming as it did close on the heels of the Venice trip. Most actors would have swallowed their pride for the honour of meeting the Royal Family.

Tony Holland, too, gave in under the pressure: at the end of 1987 he disappeared to Amsterdam, amid gossip that the had thrown in the towel and wasn't coming back. The popular papers ran stories about his gay love life – one of his ex-lovers even supplied a photograph of Julia Smith sunbathing topless on a beach, taken when she was holidaying with Tony and his lover. But the official version of Tony's departure said he was on sick leave, and, true enough, he was back in the fold in the new year. Both he and Julia (and many of the cast) had worked from the launch of the show with no more than a week's holiday at a time, and the cracks were beginning to show.

Leslie was making more enemies. An attack by him on the black actors in the show was published, claiming that he called them 'sooties', that he said the programme was turning into *Uncle Tom's Cabin*, and that he had referred to Sally Sagoe, who played Hannah Carpenter, as looking like 'a man in a frock'. The alleged remarks were all made, once again, at the off-the-record dinner he had had with three reporters in Venice. They were taken out of context – but none the less he had made them, however jocularly.

'They were said in the way people talk among friends, but when asked on the record would use totally different language and be very much more careful about how it sounded,' says one of the reporters who was present. When the comments were published Leslie denied them, saying that someone was stirring up trouble.

But Sally Sagoe, the thirty-five-year-old actress who was written out of the soap a couple of months later, believes he *did* make them. She said she knew that he often referred to blacks as 'sooties', and that she and Oscar James, who played her husband, had heard him cracking jokes about 'sooties'.

'Oscar and I were appalled. We felt embarrassed not just for ourselves but for our two screen children, Paul Medford and Delanie Forbes. Leslie later tried to deny the comments but I did not believe him. Those words were totally in character for him. I once heard him substitute a line of dialogue with a comment about "sooties", and pretend it was a joke.'

Sally also believes that Leslie was so all-powerful behind the scenes, and got on so well with producer Julia Smith, that he was not reprimanded for insulting her and Oscar – and that his dislike of them influenced their being written out. By this stage his relationship with Julia had declined, but he certainly still had a lot of clout.

'He thought he really was the kingpin,' Sally says. 'He could switch on the charm instantly, and he used it fully on Julia Smith. He was her blue-eyed boy and could do no wrong. She stood firmly by him when the facts about his killing the taxi driver were exposed. Yet she didn't spare a kind word for Oscar and me when we were victims of his cruel remarks.

'Leslie was a know-all and very off-hand with the rest of us. He used to wander in like an overseer or co- producer, and he made sure he kept his distance from us the rest of the time. He would make nasty, funny digs about other cast members. But he couldn't take a joke himself. He hated to be criticized.'

She claims, correctly, that at different times he upset Peter Dean, Shirley Cheriton and Anita Dobson.

As the time for renewal of contracts came round, there was even more speculation that Leslie was leaving the series. It was rumoured that he had been offered £3000 a week to work behind the bar of a new pub to be opened in the ailing *Crossroads* series. It was rumoured that he was selling his house and leaving to live in Australia. It was rumoured that he was going to have his own comedy series. It was even rumoured that all the rumours had been deliberately leaked by Leslie – to find out which member of the cast was tipping newspapers off about his private life. One of the females in the cast was believed to be Les's hot tip as the culprit, as he is alleged to have sent her to Coventry because of it.

Certainly, the easy relationships he had forged with the rest of the cast at the beginning were under pressure. He still had friends. Actor Allan O'Keefe – who played punk Mary's dad – rated him as not just the best actor on the show, but also the nicest bloke.

'He's a man's man. He has a laugh, a joke, sees the funny side of things. Others are up themselves – not him. And he's a complete professional, always on cue, always determined to give his best.'

But increasingly, more and more of the others had felt the cutting edge of Leslie's tongue, felt too many of the jokes were on them. There weren't too many shedding tears when he finally did make arrangements to leave the show. He had already been given time off to make a BBC-2 play, *Nightwatch*, which had whetted his appetite for work outside the soap. But the prospect of losing their central character (especially so soon after Anita Dobson had left) dismayed the *EastEnders* bosses, who bent over backwards to find ways of keeping Leslie in at least until his contract ran out in spring 1989.

He had done a deal with Scottish TV, an ITV company, to make a three-hour mini-series, *Winners and Losers*, in which he would play a cockney boxing promotor – and for which he would be paid £100,000, more than double his annual salary on *EastEnders*. There were other highly lucrative deals in the pipeline, as well as the possibility of starring in a series devised by himself and Gary Whelan, who appeared in *EastEnders* as Detective Sergeant Rich. News about their proposed series leaked out, and shortly afterwards Leslie had to call in British Telecom engineers, who found that all three telephone lines to his Fulham home were bugged.

Gary Whelan claimed that he, too, was being spied on – he said he had found a man going through the dustbins outside his Hackney home at 3 a.m. one morning. The six-foot three-inch, sixteen stone actor dealt with the 'spy' by 'bashing' him. The assumption was that he and Leslie were under observation by business rivals, out to steal their ideas for the new series. But a more sinister possible motive came to light when a showbiz minder tried to con his way round Fleet Street with stories about Leslie's private life. They were untrue and Leslie threatened to sue anyone who printed them. He has become an expert in the law of libel, having successfully sued newspapers before, and he uses a firm of solicitors who take an aggressive line over anything printed about him that is incorrect. One ex-soldier who talked for a few minutes on the telphone to a reporter about the time that Leslie was arrested in Germany received a solicitor's letter telling him to desist from further communications with the media. It cost the ex-soldier a trip to his own solicitor to discover that Leslie had no power to stop him talking as long as he told the truth. But that letter, coupled with the threatening phone calls that the ex-soldier and his family received from fans, effectively frightened him off ever talking again.

But Fleet Street has kept a pretty close eye on Leslie Grantham since he became Britain's biggest soap star, and his paranoia about the press is not entirely without foundation.

Another reason that Leslie wanted to leave *EastEnders* was that Jane was expecting their second baby, and he wanted more free time to spend with his family. The baby, another boy, named Jake, arrived in September 1988. Like his older brother, he was born at the Portland Hospital, the exclusive private hospital where only weeks before Fergie had given birth to Princess Beatrice.

Instead of writing him out of the series finally, the scriptwriters capitalized as never before on his past.

Julia Smith and Tony Holland devised a way of milking his departure to their best possible advantage, and keeping him on screen for as long as possible. They decided to send him to prison. He was accused of arson, the Dagmar pub having been burned to the ground. He had left the Queen Vic by then; Angie (Anita Dobson) had been written out, having divorced Den and gone to Spain with another man; and even the dog Roly had been handed over to the new landlord at the Vic (comedian-turned-actor Mike Reid).

It meant that in a couple of weeks of intensive filming they were able to make enough self-contained prison inserts to keep slipping Den into the show for months. It cleverly left the door open for him to reappear whenever he chooses, a safety net that he is grateful for, having not quite found the courage to fly the coop completely.

The filming was done in a wing of Dartmoor that was closed for redecoration. They were strong scenes: Den learning how to handle life behind bars, how prisoners treat sex offenders, how they treat gays, futile interviews with welfare workers and psychiatrists.

It was, for Den Watts, a rerun of Leslie Grantham's own experiences, cynically milked by the scriptwriters for maximum impact. It was Leslie's prison background that boosted ratings at the beginning of the series. At the end of his time in it, when the show was battling hard against the cheap Australian soap *Neighbours* for top billing in the ratings, it was his prison background that was exploited again, leaving the indelible image of him as a hard-faced loner with survival on his mind.

Was it Den – or was it Leslie? It was a confusion that worked well for the show, and one that Leslie was happy to go along with. Despite his professed anguish when newspapers have raked over the coals of his past life, when it suits him he is happy to capitalize on it. And if it helped revitalize public interest in him at a time when he was trying to launch himself to stardom away from *EastEnders*, he was up for it.

CHAPTER 11

Widow Reese and Family

What happened to Liesel Reese in the years that Leslie Grantham was finding riches and celebrity as Britain's biggest-ever soap star? How did the widow of the taxi driver he shot cope with life after the death of her husband?

Not easily. After the initial shock of Felix's death wore off, Liesel became acutely aware of her poverty. Although the house she lived in was her parents', they could not afford to pay the mortgage without some income from the flat upstairs. Liesel still had to pay rent, or the whole family would have lost their home. So she was desperately short of money.

When the reward money was offered to the boxer who turned Leslie Grantham in, he refused to accept it, but asked that it should be given to the widow. It wasn't. It simply wasn't paid out at all – a fact that today shocks the boxer, who has lived all these years in the belief that the money went to Liesel and Kirsten. The money collected by the taxi drivers would have helped Liesel, but she was determined to put it away for Kirsten's future, which she did.

Kirsten was five when her father died. Liesel's first reaction was to start work again full time, leaving Kirsten with her mother. She went back to the weaving mill where she had worked before Kirsten was born. But German children do not start school until they are seven, so the strain on Frau Weilage, who was no longer young, and Liesel's love for her little daughter meant that she was only able to work full time for eight months after Felix's death.

'I felt Kirsten was all I had left, and I was missing seeing her grow up. I wanted to be with her badly, but when I got home from the mill I was tired and she was tired. Sometimes my mother would have put her to bed, so I didn't see her at all except in the mornings. It was no good. I gave up my job. I thought I would rather be poor and spend some time with Kirsten, who was all I had left of Felix.'

So she gave up full-time work and started cleaning for two hours a day, at a rate of 5DM (43p) an hour. Liesel was proud, and refused to seek charity. She made all Kirsten's clothes, and her own, out of cheap material. She unpicked old jumpers and knitted them up again for her daughter. Felix had loved meat, but Liesel and Kirsten grew used to eating only vegetables, cooked in stock from meat bones. There were no little extras for Kirsten, no presents when daddy came home, no sweets. The chubby little girl soon became a skinny kid.

Having her parents downstairs helped to allay loneliness. But Liesel says today: 'There is no loneliness like the loneliness you feel when you have really loved a man and he is not there. Friends and family cannot fill that emptiness.'

And there was a double blow. Exactly a year after the murder, her father died of cancer. He was ill for a few months, so Liesel had to help her mother nurse him. Liesel had come to rely on him. After Felix's death her father had taken over his duties in the garden, had done any odd jobs that his daughter needed doing, and had taught her how to handle her own affairs – paying bills and so on. Now both she and her mother were widows, with a house to run and maintain and pay for on their very low pensions.

As soon as Kirsten started at school, Liesel increased

the hours she worked. She not only did domestic cleaning in someone's house, but she also cleaned a shop and worked part-time in a pub, helping in the kitchens.

'There was never any money left by the end of the month. The last week of the month was always bad. I couldn't afford new tights, and often went without any. When Kirsten started school I realized just how poor we were. I had to buy her uniform and her books, and there wasn't enough money. But Kirsten wanted the same things as the other children – she didn't want secondhand things. So I struggled, and we cut down elsewhere. With my father dead my mother had no money to spare. Felix's family kept in touch, but his brothers and sisters had children of their own to bring up, and his parents had no money, either.

'Looking back, I don't know how I kept going. I couldn't do it now. I learned to decorate the flat myself, I learned to change plugs. You cannot always be asking friends to help. I felt I had to be father and mother to Kirsten, and it was a strain. Most of all, I missed company: someone to talk through my day with in bed at night.'

Kirsten soon realized that birthday and Christmas presents would be clothes – things she needed, not things she wanted. There was no money left over for toys.

'One year, when she was about ten, there was a lot of ice and all her friends had ice skates. She desperately wanted some. She was very good – she rarely asked me for anything. So when she asked for the skates I said I would buy them as soon as I had saved the 20DM (£4) that I needed. By the time I had saved it, the ice had melted.

'Kirsten got used to her friends having bikes and other expensive presents. She never grumbled or made me feel bad. She understood why things were so bad for us. We would talk about her papa as she lay in bed at night. It would make her happy to believe he was in heaven watching her. But it would upset me, and after I left her I would go in the sitting room and cry.'

For the first couple of years after the murder the Osnabrück taxi drivers kept in touch, calling round to see how Liesel was getting on and bringing her small presents. But as the memory of the murder faded, the visits dropped off. 'After all, they were Felix's friends, not mine,' says Liesel.

She tried to keep up her social life at the shooting club, and members would make sure she was invited – free – to all their events. But Liesel was constantly aware that all the others there were in couples, and that she was the odd one out. She also felt embarrassed by her lack of nice, new clothes, like the other women had. Gradually she stopped going.

As the sixties progressed into the seventies, all their friends started to have holidays abroad. It was the era when foreign travel for all boomed: and it boomed more in prosperous West Germany than anywhere else in Europe. The statutory two weeks in the sun became part of the German way of life. But not for Liesel and Kirsten. Liesel would take time off work when Kirsten was off school, and the two of them would go swimming – to the same pool where Liesel and Felix met.

They would also make excursions to Schinkel cemetery, where Felix was buried. Only a ten-minute walk from the flat, it is a very pretty cemetery where, in German tradition, 99 per cent of the graves are carefully tended, with an assortment of seasonal plants always in bloom. The walkways are clean and paved, and the fields of graves are irregular in layout, with taps and water troughs at intervals for the use of the gardeners. At any time of the day, men and women with small rakes and spades and watering cans can be

seen digging and weeding and watering the plots of
their loved ones.

Like most Germans, Liesel only bought the grave for
twenty years. Though they tend the graves assiduously
while they are there, Germans are pragmatic enough to
accept that after twenty years there is precious little left of
their dead relatives, and they allow the graves to be
bulldozed and the land used again for new burials. They
express surprise that anyone would do otherwise, or in
any way think their system odd. Married couples with
children often buy a grave for forty years – the maximum
allowed, although once you have it it can be extended –
which means they can both be buried there. But the
undertakers advised Liesel against this, as Felix was so
young when he died and it was unlikely that she would
die within forty years. Georg Liekam's taxi company paid
for the funeral, and would have been prepared to pay for
the family plot. But Liesel decided against it.

Liesel tended Felix's grave once a week – on Sundays
– during the winter, and twice or three times a week
during the summer. She would call there on her way
home from work to water the geraniums and begonias
she planted every summer. In the winter, the ferns and
small shrubs needed less attention.

Eventually, when she found the confidence to start
socializing again, Liesel began to go out on dates with
other men, leaving her mother to babysit. But the
relationships did not last. She found nobody who
measured up to Felix, and she was frightened of becoming too involved because she did not want Kirsten
to have a stepfather.

'You can never be sure how a man who is not the
natural father will treat a child. Kirsten was my main
consideration. And besides, I never felt close enough to
anyone to want to share my life with him.'

When Kirsten was twelve, Liesel showed her the
newspaper cuttings about her father's murder.

'I already knew how he had died, but it wasn't until I read the old newspapers that I really understood the details,' says Kirsten. 'Mama just left me alone to go through them, and I cried and cried. Even today, I take them out and I cry. It seems I cry more each time. People say things get better over the years, but I don't believe that. I feel the loss of my father acutely, all the time.'

At school there were two incidents that stick in her memory. One was when the children in the schoolyard were miming their fathers' occupations, and a boy turned to Kirsten and said, 'You'd better pretend to be dead.' The other was in class, when the four girls who shared a table and were best friends – Kirsten, Roswithe, Bettina and Petra – were discussing what their fathers did. Petra turned to Kirsten and said, 'You can't join in – you haven't got a father.'

Both times Kirsten went home and cried.

'When I got older I missed having nice clothes a lot. But I never blamed mama. I knew she always tried her hardest and gave me the best of what we had. I would daydream all the time about how life would have been different if papa had lived, and how perhaps I would have had a younger brother or sister to play with. And how there would always have been money, and we would have had holidays and I could have had a bike like everybody else. But they were only dreams.'

When she was sixteen Kirsten left school and took up an apprenticeship with a local baker and confectioner. A year before she left school, Liesel took up full-time work in a factory that makes reinforced glass booths – the sort used in banks or post offices. The work involves her lifting and carrying large sheets of glass and plastic, and cutting them on electric saws. It is heavy manual work, which after tax earns Liesel 800DM (£258) a month.

Because the factory is on the Schinkel industrial

estate it is only five minutes' walk from Liesel's home. Liesel has never learned to drive because she could never afford a car. She hates travelling by taxi, so whenever she wants to shop in the city centre she has to use buses.

With Kirsten also earning, at last the family finances began to look up. Kirsten has grown up into a loose-limbed girl, five feet eight inches tall, with the same dark hair and eyes as her mother. She is a very animated girl, laughing a lot and talking all the time. Her mother is much quieter and very neatly dressed. She spends all her spare time knitting complicated and beautiful cobweb-pattern jumpers and tops. The two are very close.

'Kirsten is like her father – she never stops singing or laughing. She reminds me of him so much that it hurts. Her facial expressions are like his, and the way she moves is like him. And like him she is happy-go-lucky,' says Liesel.

In 1987, Liesel and Kirsten suffered a serious blow – the discovery that Leslie Grantham was not only out of prison, but was a big star in Britain. It was a reporter from a British newspaper who broke the news to them, and it heralded another few months of trauma. It had genuinely never occurred to Liesel that her husband's murderer would be set free: she had naïvely assumed that a 'life' sentence meant imprisonment for life.

'After years of having nightmares about Felix's death I had, for three or four years, been able to sleep without tablets and without bad dreams. Suddenly, after that phone call from the reporter, all the bad dreams came flooding back. I had to go to my doctor to get more sleeping tablets. Kirsten was very upset, too. We would be sitting talking together and then one of us would suddenly burst into tears. It brought everything back.'

Shortly after the first phone call, journalists began to

appear on Liesel's doorstep. She was obliging and prepared to talk about her feelings. And despite the fact that reliving Felix's death was distressing, the happy corollary was that British newspapers were prepared to pay her for interviews.

The first reaction of both Liesel and Kirsten to the news that Leslie Grantham was a highly paid star was to think in terms of their own poverty, each believing that he should have made some reparation to the other. Liesel said he should make a substantial payment to Kirsten, to help set her up in life and in some small way compensate her for the loss of all the material things she had missed out on as a child. Kirsten, on the other hand, believed that her mother should be compensated for her miserable life without a husband she had loved.

But despite the massive publicity given to their story, no payment was forthcoming. So the two women feel more than justified taking cheques from newspapers: they have been paid more than £10,000 altogether. The money has substantially improved their lives. Until the cheques started to arrive, they still lived in the tiny, cramped flat above Frau Weilage's, using the same furniture that Liesel and Felix had so carefully scraped together the money to buy. The house was over thirty years old and beginning to need work, but neither Liesel nor her elderly mother downstairs could afford it. The balcony leading off Liesel's sitting room was leaking damp into the flat below. With the newspaper money Liesel was able to have her sitting room extended, making the balcony part of the room. It cured the damp, and more than doubled the size of Liesel's sitting room, which is now spacious, light and airy. There was enough money over to refurnish the flat with tasteful modern furniture, and also to provide Kirsten with money for the home that she and her husband-to-be set up.

But perhaps the most distressing piece of news that a

British journalist brought to them was the news that Felix's skull was not in the grave at Schinkel cemetery, but was the centrepiece of a display on crimes committed by soldiers at a training centre for military police at the Royal Military Police museum at Roussillon barracks in Chichester, Sussex.

'Of course, I knew that the skull was an exhibit at the trial, and that was long after we buried Felix. But I never thought about what happened to it. Somehow in my mind I have always thought all of him was in the grave. I was terribly upset to hear that the skull was an exhibit in a museum,' says Liesel.

As soon as Leslie Grantham and his lawyers heard that the skull was on display, they wrote to the museum and it was immediately withdrawn from view. The *Sun* offered to pay for it to be shipped back to Germany and buried with the rest of Felix's remains. But by then it was August 1986 – less than four months from the end of Liesel's rental of the burial plot.

'There did not seem any sense in having it brought here,' she says. 'I simply didn't want it on display. I do not really believe that it is important. Felix's soul is in heaven, and that is what counts.'

The *Sun* also offered to pay for Liesel to rent the burial plot for longer – but that was impossible, as Felix's grave was in a field of graves all due to be bulldozed at the same time. Liesel concurs with the German belief that after twenty years nothing physical remains of her husband, and whilst having a deep sentimental attachment to his memory, she does not value very highly the piece of land in which he was laid to rest.

She was notified in the spring of 1987 that the grave was due to be bulldozed the following autumn. She was given six months' notice, so that she could remove any plants or the headstone. But Liesel simply went on maintaining the grave until the day the bulldozers moved in.

'I was not there to see it. I have been back to the cemetery since, because my father and brother-in-law are both buried there. But I walk quickly past the field where Felix used to be. I try not to look.'

After graves are bulldozed, the headstones are kept for a year in case the family wish to claim them. Felix's headstone, which said simply: 'Felix Reese – In Loving Memory', was not claimed. Liesel says she has nowhere to keep it, and does not like the thought of it in the garden. The field where the grave used to be was reseeded in the spring of 1988, and about a year after that was due to be used again as a burial ground.

Since 1986 Liesel has had her only two holidays after the death of her husband. Her first, a week in a holiday resort on the Baltic coast in 1985, was not a great success.

'Unlike Felix and Kirsten, I am not a happy-go-lucky person. Being on my own, I find it hard to make contact with others. I felt very isolated. In the end I did make some friends – I talked to some married couples. But I felt strange.'

Two years ago she had a holiday partly paid for by the West German National Health Service. Because of the heavy work that she does all day in the factory, Liesel has problems with her back. She went to stay in Bad Gögging, near Munich, close to the Austrian border, at a spa centre specially equipped with hydrotherapy pools, physiotherapy rooms and medical experts. Because of her condition all the treatments she received were free, but she had to pay for her own travel and subsidized accommodation. She enjoyed her week there, and felt that the treatments had done her good.

'My backache improved for some months. But I have to carry on with the work, and I now have the pain

179

again. I will have to work until I am sixty because if I stop any sooner I will get only a tiny pension – as it is, it will be small because I have not worked full-time for enough years. So I have another ten years of hard work ahead of me. I would like to find a lighter job, but there just aren't any available. I am not trained for office work. If Felix had lived, I would have spent my life very happily as a housewife.'

In 1983 Kirsten met the man who is now her husband, thirty-three-year-old Heinz Simon, a construction engineer who builds industrial hangars. But Liesel had started saving for her daughter's wedding long before.

'As soon as she left school and I was working full-time I started putting money away for the wedding,' says Liesel. 'It is traditional in this country for the bride's parents to pay, and I have always known that Felix would have wanted his daughter to have the best wedding possible. Besides, both of Heinz's parents are dead, so they could not help.'

In the German tradition, Kirsten and Heinz had two wedding ceremonies: the first, in a register office, several months earlier than the second, full celebration after a ceremony in church. The wedding day was 23 September 1988, Kirsten's twenty-seventh birthday, at St Jacobus Protestant church. Kirsten would like to have married in the same church as her mother, but since her civil wedding she and Heinz have moved into a rented flat in a different area of the city, and they have to marry in the parish they live in.

The celebrations cost over 6500DM (£2,100). The wedding dress alone, a full-length traditional white one cost 1000DM (£320). Fifty-eight people, most of them family, attended the reception – a meal and dance in a local hall. German wedding guests give not presents but money, which is traditionally counted at the reception by the parents of the bride and groom.

'Out of the four parents I am the only one alive, so I had to do all the organizing and all the counting,' says Liesel, 'But now that it is over and Kirsten is happy, at last I do not have to save. All my life it has been save, save, save. When Felix was alive we would talk about the days when he would have his own taxi business and there would be money for everything. He always told me the saving would pay off. Well, now it has. I have managed to give Kirsten a wedding day to remember. I am proud of her, and proud that I managed it.'

She has not been lonely since Kirsten, who now works as a telephonist for an advertising agency, moved out. 'It seemed strange at first, but because Heinz works away from home during the week she often comes here after work. And I see them both every weekend. Kirsten telephones me, too, all the time.'

Since the death of her brother-in-law, Liesel's sister has moved into the downstairs flat with their mother, so she is not short of company. Frau Weilage is now elderly and frail, so the sisters are kept busy looking after her.

Both Liesel and Kirsten are left with a genuine sense of deep outrage that Leslie Grantham, who shattered their lives so profoundly, can have risen to be a wealthy top star as well as a happy family man. They are both at pains to point out that they have no grudge against the British. Kirsten is a great fan of the British Royal Family and would love to visit London. Liesel believes that all nations have a percentage of what she calls 'bad people' – and that Leslie Grantham is one of the British ones.

'I do not hate the British. It was British soldiers who turned him in. They could not stand what he had done, either. People are the same, whatever country they are from. But I do not believe in my country he would have risen to such fame.

'I know I ought to believe that he has served his

sentence, and therefore is free to lead his life however he can. But I would have thought for decency's sake, having done what he did, he would keep out of the limelight. A colleague of mine at work asked me if I would like to see a video of him. I do not want to see him ever again. Kirsten said she would punch a hole in the television set if she ever saw him on it, and I believe she would. She is much more vitriolic than I am.

'I wonder sometimes about his wife and family. His wife said she did not care what he had done in the past. How can she not care? We are all the result of what we have done in the past – there isn't any escape from it. She may have reconciled herself to it, but I don't believe she doesn't care about it.

'And his children: how is he going to tell them what he did? I bet he will gloss over it and never tell them the full story of how he shot my Felix in cold blood. I don't wish any harm on children – it is not their fault, any more than it was his parents' fault. So I don't mind if they never know the truth if it would harm them. But I think he does not face up to the truth, and that is bad.

'He and his wife are now at the stage that Felix and I were at when Felix was murdered. Sure, they have a lot more money and material things. But like us they are facing a happy future bringing up their family. How would Leslie Grantham feel if that was suddenly pulled away from him, through no fault of his?

'When I lie awake at night thinking about it all, I wonder whether he is also lying awake, perhaps thinking about me. But I don't suppose so. He has managed to shut all thought of me and my shattered life out of his mind all these years. So why should he worry now?'

CHAPTER 12

The Other Granthams

They had been an ordinary family, with ordinary hopes and aspirations, until that phone call in 1966 to tell them that their middle son, Leslie, had been arrested for murder. Since then, the rest of the Grantham family have had to struggle to lead normal lives. As Leslie's sister Angela puts it, it is as though 'from that day on, thanks to Leslie, we were destined to be different. Nothing was ever the same again.'

Angela remembers with pain having to explain to her fiancé's family what had happened. She also remembers how the report of the verdict was splashed across the front of the *Daily Sketch*, and how when she travelled by train to work she knew that people were nudging and whispering and pointing her out to each other. She offered her future husband the chance to break off their engagement, but he refused. The wedding went ahead when Angela was eighteen, only a few months after Leslie's trial. It was a big family affair at St Mary's church, St Mary Cray, with a reception afterwards at the Liberal Hall. Leslie sent a greetings telegram. It was perhaps ironic that it was in the year after he and Angela married that Graham McNab decided to join the police.

Wally and Anne Grantham were undemonstrative as usual, but they liked Graham and they were pleased when the first of Angela's two children, her daughter Claire, was born two years after Les went to prison. At last the family seemed to be back on some sort of even

183

keel. Apart from the regular visits to Wormwood Scrubs, their lives were almost normal again.

They went twice a month to see Leslie. Usually John and his girlfriend Anne did one visit and Wally and Anne – often with Philip or Angela – did the other. They received regular letters home from Leslie, and despite the fact that his handwriting 'looks like a steamroller ran over his hand', according to brother John, their content was light and cheerful. John believes that the years in the army had been a good preparation for prison life, and that Leslie adjusted easily to the harsh institutional regime.

John finished his apprenticeship and worked as a printer with the *Kentish Times* for twelve months. But he did not enjoy the job: his main pleasure from work came when he was serving behind the bar of the Seven Stiles, which he still did in the evenings and at weekends. After the court martial verdict he had offered to resign because of the local interest in the story, but, like Graham with Angela, the Huggetts stood by him and refused. He remembers local people, too, being supportive and kind.

But others who knew him at the time remember that John was acutely embarrassed by his brother's crime. When he was asked how Leslie was getting on he would answer brusquely and change the subject.

'We got the impression it was something he would rather not talk about,' says Richard Tugwell, who served behind the bar with John and now manages a pub. 'John was a great bloke who taught me all I know about running a bar. He was a natural at it. And normally he was very chatty. But if you asked him about Leslie he would clam up. He wanted to forget all about it.'

Wally Grantham resolutely never gave up his Sunday lunchtime pint at the pub, but his aura of fierce pride prevented anyone from raising the subject of Leslie with him. Anne Grantham spent a few weeks after the trial not venturing out of the house, although eventually she resumed her regular habit of popping into the off-licence to buy cigarettes.

Having left the printing trade, John became manager first of a bingo hall in Peckham and then of a branch of Cosmos Tours travel agency. On Saturdays his younger brother Philip, by now in the sixth form at Bromley Grammar School and doing well, worked with him in the shop. Like all the Grantham children, Philip always worked for his pocket money, at one time doing a round delivering paraffin. He was so reliable that the travel agency shop could be left entirely in his hands for hours at a time. Philip took the news of Leslie's sentence very hard: he was quieter and more sensitive than the others. He used the money he earned to pay his own fares to visit Leslie, whom he had idolized as a child.

In the family tradition Philip was a tall, good-looking youngster, very popular at school. In the upper sixth he was made head boy, and after passing his A levels he went to Manchester University to read American History. When his three-year degree course was completed he did not invite his parents to his graduation ceremony. He told his sister that he had got as far as he had despite them, not because of them, and they were not going to share his triumph. He had certainly had to struggle to find a quiet space to do his homework, sharing a bedroom as he did first with Angela and then with John, and working against the constant background of bickering that characterized the Grantham home.

He stayed at university for another year to do his Diploma of Education, the qualification needed to teach. His first job was teaching history in a Manchester school, but he did not enjoy it much. By this time Manchester had gone comprehensive, and Philip found himself teaching children of all ability ranges. He complained that they were not interested in learning.

For three of the years that he lived in Manchester he shared a flat with a girl called Hilary, whom his family met and liked. Hilary helped allay any creeping fears that Philip preferred men to women: to this day his father and his brother John insist that Philip was normal and heterosexual. But the relationship with Hilary was purely platonic. By this time Philip, at least, knew that he was homosexual. Angela and her mother both suspected it, but it wasn't until a few years later that they were sure.

'It began to emerge in little ways, little details,' says Angela. 'Although he always looked and dressed macho, he had a very neat, orderly world. It was a nice world – Philip always surrounded himself with nice things and friends. He knew plenty of girls, but they were not girlfriends. He had a brilliant sense of humour – much the best in the family – and he was a great mimic. He could do Joan Crawford, Bette Davis and Humphrey Bogart so well you'd have sworn it was them. He should have been the star – he was the one with the talent. Everyone who knew him says that.'

Philip gave up teaching and joined Cosmos Tours again, working in branches in Edinburgh, Bristol and London. Eventually he was put in charge of their whole US division, and he pioneered the installation of an advanced computer system. He was subsequently head-hunted by a rival tour company.

Angela had a second baby, a son called Alex, in 1971, and she and Graham were living happily enough in Sundridge Park in a police house. Most of her spare time as a teenager had been spent cooking and cleaning for her family, so the transition to married life was not hard. She didn't feel, as many young girls do who are pampered by their mothers, that she was missing out by being married. If anything her workload was reduced, with fewer shirts to iron each week.

John, in the meantime, had married his first wife, Anne, when he was twenty-four. It lasted two years. John believes it foundered because he was working too hard at the travel agency.

'The last thing I took was a holiday myself, I just sold them to other people. I was working evenings, weekends. I didn't know when to stop. Anne and I were in love and well suited – she visited Les with me and they go on well. But in the end she got fed up with my working hours. She had a job with Unilever which gave her the chance to go to Africa for six months, and while she was there she met someone else. *Boom*. That was that.'

John took refuge in his favourite place – the pub. When, in 1974, Wally Grantham was offered a job at the branch of Boots in Farnborough, Hampshire, he and Anne got a council house transfer and moved away from Tillingbourne Green. John followed them. Four years after their move he found himself a job working on the production line at the Johnsons Wax factory making furniture polish. Within a few months of starting there he met his second wife, Wendy, who worked on the night shift with him. Wendy had been married before and had four children, but the children divided their time between her and their father.

Wendy and John settled down into a routine that suited them both, however unhealthy it subsequently proved to be. After the night shift they would sleep for a few hours, then go to the pub for a few drinks at lunchtime, sleep again in the afternoon, and then have a few more drinks before going on to their shift on the production line. They lived in a council flat, and their combined earnings gave them over £300 a week – enough for occasional holidays with all Wendy's kids at Butlins.

Although John's life had perhaps not worked out as well as they had hoped, and they talked within the family about him drinking too much, he was still the apple of Wally and Anne's eye. Wally would join him for a drink every Sunday lunchtime.

The visits to Les continued. When he was in Kingston Prison, in Portsmouth, John would combine a visit with a trip to the Isle of Wight for the weekend. Although it was further for them to travel than Wormwood Scrubs, they were all relieved that Leslie was living in better conditions, and Anne was pleased to see him lose his prison pallor and begin to look healthy.

Ley Hill was even further for them to go, but they never purposely missed a visit. Leslie's uncle John Flinders, his mother's brother, travelled from Manchester to see him, and his father's sister Joan and her husband Ernie Touchert also came from Camberwell. Later, when he was released from prison, he stayed with them for a time. On one occasion Anne got on the wrong train and ended up in Wales, having no alternative but to turn round and return home, missing her visit. Such potential problems were avoided on the occasions when Angela and Graham drove them there; Wally paid for the petrol.

Staff at Ley Hill remember being warned that Leslie was always upset when his mother came to visit. Not knowing her, they believed it was because she made him feel guilty about the shame he had brought on the family.

'I think mum was never as comforting as dad because she wouldn't let Les get away with anything,' says Angela. 'She could see through Les. Dad never could. His pride blinded him. Les has got this huge chip on his shoulder about his family, and we don't know where it came from, because he didn't have a worse upbringing than the rest of us. In fact, he got away with a lot more as a kid than I ever did. And when he was in prison his family supported him.'

Perhaps the constant introspection of the psychiatrists' sessions and the group therapy at Kingston had taught Leslie to look deeply into his own past to find motivation for his deeds and rationale for his situation. If that is the case, Angela believes he looked too deeply.

'You cannot blame your parents for what you do. It may not have been a perfect childhood – whose is? But it was no different for the rest of us, and we didn't get into trouble. Les takes the view that everyone and everything was against him, but it just isn't true. We have discussed it many times, and none of us can understand where he gets it from. We all grew up in the same environment, after all.'

Wally and Anne had one exciting holiday to take their minds off family problems. Anne's sister Daphne, ten years younger, had married an American, Oswald Singletary, when he was over in Britain with the American forces in the years after the war. Osie, as Oswald is known, and Daphne used to live in Baton Rouge, Lousiana, where Osie worked as a state trooper. His family owned land and property, so he and Daphne had a lifestyle far removed from the council estate in Tillingbourne Green. They breed palomino horses for a hobby, and Daphne runs an antiques and crafts business, buying up stocks on her visits to Britain. Since Osie's retirement the couple now live in Slidell, near New Orleans. But at the time that Anne and Wally travelled out to stay with them, they were living on a ranch outside Baton Rouge. Unfortunately, the dream holiday had to be cut short by the news that Wally's sister had died.

Wally retired from Boots in 1981, and was rewarded with a presentation for long service. The family, and John in particular, were worried that work had occupied such a major part of his life that he would find retirement difficult.

'I predicted he would be dead from boredom within six months,' says John. To the astonishment and delight of them all, Wally took up driving, passed his test first time, and stood for election to the local Rushmoor District Council, as a Tory councillor. He got in, despite tough local opposition.

Three years earlier Leslie had come out of prison, and he was now making his way as an actor. The family knew there was always a risk that his background would come out, and both Angela and his mother were surprised that he had chosen to go into a job where he was thrusting himself into the spotlight. But they were all pleased and proud when things began to work out for him. Leslie himself was well aware of the risks of bad publicity. Soon after starting at drama school he visited his parents' home and removed all photographs of himself. His mother was annoyed, because many of them were the only ones she had of her family together.

So when, in February 1985, the blow came, the family were half expecting it. *EastEnders* had been launched, and the stories about Leslie's past were plastered all over the popular newspapers. '*EastEnders* star is convicted killer', the headlines ran. It was not too long before journalists tracked down Liesel Reese in Osnabrück, and 'Dirty Den Ruined Our Lives' screamed the banner headlines.

'When he got the part in *EastEnders* the whole family held its breath,' says John. 'It was nearly twenty years since it happened, and it seemed so long ago I really believed there was a chance it would stay buried. But less than one week after the show hit the air, the news was out.'

On the night the story was due to break, Leslie rang his mother and father and warned them. They in turn rang their other three children. John went on night duty at the Pledge polish factory, and in the early hours of the morning his foreman – ironically, a German – drove to the station to pick up an early copy of the *Sun*.

'Even though I knew it was coming it was a bit of a shock, seeing it so big,' says John. 'I didn't really worry for myself, but I was worried for mum and dad, and obviously for Leslie.'

Anne Grantham was so upset that, as after the court martial, she did not leave her home for two weeks. Wally Grantham, used to walking with his head held high, again refused to capitulate and braved it out. At Leslie's instigation none of his family talked to the press.

'We got used to panic phone calls from him over the next few years, always telling us to say nothing,' says Angela. 'The worst thing for Mum is that she hasn't even been allowed to tell people how proud she is of his success.'

The news that he was a convicted killer in real life seemed to have had a perverse affect on the viewers. Dirty Den's standing grew and his role in the soap became bigger and bigger, until he and his screen wife Anita Dobson were the major focus of attention.

After the initial furore about his brother's past had died down, John began to enjoy it. He, like his father, is inordinately proud of Leslie, to the point of having tunnel vision about him. And as well as that, being Dirty Den's brother gave him a certain cachet down at his local that he revelled in. Behind the bar of the pub where he regularly drinks, a tray bears a large sign that reads: 'Dirty Den's brother drinks here.' And at any time John can produce a handful of promotional photographs of Leslie from his jacket pocket.

But John's life was not going well. After seven years of working night shifts at the polish factory, and spending almost all his free time in the pub, he had a nervous breakdown. He denies that it was caused by his brother's fame, although it followed close on the heels of the sudden swell of publicity about Leslie only four months after *EastEnders* was launched.

'The only way Leslie contributed was that I should have gone to hospital sooner than I did. I tried to keep out of hospital because of the effect of the publicity on him. I simply had a complete breakdown: I woke up one morning and I couldn't talk, walk or think even. It was as if something went ping in my head. I had to lie down again, and when I did get up I was shambling about like an old man. I had been working nights for seven years, which is not a good idea. I hadn't been taking holidays, and when I felt ill I used to just swallow Anadin and carry on. I was drinking in the morning and at night. My marriage wasn't really working out, but I was struggling not to admit it.'

Eventually John was admitted to Frimley Park Mental Hospital for three months. He felt suicidal, and was desperate that he would lose his job and end up living in a hospital forever. He panicked and discharged himself, but when he went to his local building society branch to draw out some money he was convinced the girl behind the counter was looking at him suspiciously.

'I had enough wits to realize I was being paranoid, so I took myself straight back to the hospital.'

While he was in there, Leslie visited him eleven times, bringing him cigarettes and sweets and signing endless autographs for other patients. John believes it was his patience and tolerance that helped him through. Once, when he was unable to visit, his wife Jane came – a surprise for John, who did not even recognize her at first.

'Les would sit and talk to me at the restaurant end of the ward, telling me to take things more easily, make sure I got my holidays – all that stuff. All the family rallied round, and after three months I was able to leave the hospital and go back to work, just like before.'

The hospital stay may have cured his breakdown, but it did nothing to help his failing marriage. Wendy had switched to working days, so the couple were not seeing so much of each other. When they took in a lodger – nicknamed Tricky Ricky – it was not long before Wendy and he began an affair. A nasty court case ensued, in which Wendy tried to get possession of the council flat. The court found in favour of John, and he magnanimously agreed to her and Ricky staying there until they found a place of their own. It caused headlines.

'It wasn't as peculiar as it sounds. I never really saw them, what with them working days and me working nights. And I kept my own bedroom. At first they slept in the living room, which was inconvenient. But when they moved into the other bedroom I didn't mind. It was worse when they finally moved out. I found I was nine months in arrears with the gas, the electricity and the phone, which I had to pay off.'

The phone was eventually disconnected. John was banned from driving for drinking. And he was made redundant by the polish factory.

But John's misfortunes pale into insignificance beside the story of Philip's death. Until Leslie's success on television, Philip was the high-flyer of the family, the one with the executive job and the glamorous lifestyle. His job meant that he had the opportunity to travel the world, and he did.

With the exception of his father and John, the family accepted his homosexuality. Leslie did not approve: he has never made any secret of his dislike of gays, a feeling that was reinforced by his prison years when he witnessed homosexual activities at close quarters. Whenever he asked his sister Angela about Philip he would say, 'Is he still living in fairyland?' Or 'Is he still away with the fairies?' To the others it was an open secret: they did not discuss it. Angela knew that at one time her brother lived with another man, but she did not know any details.

'Philip accepted that I knew, and yet we didn't talk about it. He had his life. He was a good brother and an excellent uncle to my children,' said Angela. 'He had lots of friends and he was very happy. That was all that mattered.'

Until Aids. Although Philip's friends maintain that he was not promiscuous, he had undoubtedly had quite a few sexual encounters. He lived in his own flat in West Kensington, near to the Fulham and Chelsea areas that he loved, and his circle of friends were all gay. He also travelled on holidays to the Far East, where it is possible that he made homosexual contacts in the notorious gay bars. Perhaps inevitably, he contracted the HIV-positive virus, which developed into full-blown Aids.

His death at St Mary's Hospital, Westminster on 7 October 1986 was attributed on his death certificate to pneumonia, a common cause of death among Aids victims, who are not killed by the Aids virus itself but by the resultant lack of resistance to other infections. It is also common not to use the word 'Aids' on the death certificate, and was particularly so in 1986 when the Aids epidemic was comparatively new. Lack of understanding about the means by which the virus is spread has led to some victims being refused normal burial and cremation rights, and families are anxious to avoid the obvious stigma. Doctors and hospitals co-operate by not naming the HIV-positive virus as a secondary cause of death.

This has made it possible for Wally and John – and subsequently Leslie – to assert that Philip did not die of Aids. However, months before his death he had himself told his family the nature of the disease he was suffering from. For months he was in and out of hospital, and his weight dwindled. He sold his flat and moved in with two friends of his, Simon and Ian, who lived in Chelsea and who looked after him solicitously. At weekends he would travel to Sundridge Park to stay with Angela and her family, where John and his mother and father would visit him. He remained light-hearted and jokey, even about his condition. John remembers him being touchingly grateful for a present of Pledge furniture polish.

Anne Grantham would have liked Philip to live at home, where she could have nursed him properly. But he preferred not to go. He wanted to stay with his friends in the area he loved, and he also wanted to spare his parents the embarrassment of neighbours and friends finding out about his condition. With his father a local councillor and his brother a famous television star, Philip was all too aware of the sensitivity of his illness, and at one stage even asked St Mary's Hospital to change his surname on their files.

His last few months were painful, but peaceful. His sister Angela spent a lot of time with him, and he confided in her that he would not change anything if he could lead his life again. He had led a happy and, in his terms, fulfilled life, and he was prepared to die with equanimity.

But there was one great disappointment for him, as death approached. His brother Leslie, of whom he, too, was so proud, did not visit him. In the weeks that the family knew Philip was dying, Leslie made only one phone call to him: a very brief one in which he told Philip he was just trying out his car phone and would ring again later. He never did.

When Leslie was told of Philip's illness, his reaction was not one of concern for Philip. According to Angela, he said: 'That's another f—ing nail in my coffin.'

195

'Philip was very hurt that Leslie rejected him,' said Angela, 'He could not understand how someone who could take a life, and serve all those years in prison, could look down on someone else just because they were gay. Phil was gentle and kind and he couldn't understand it: he himself had never rejected Leslie. We also knew that now Leslie had a showbusiness background he must be rubbing shoulders with lots of gays, and we were surprised that it didn't make him more tolerant. Every time the phone rang, when Philip was staying at my house at the weekends, he would think it was Leslie. He would look up hopefully, and I'd have to say, "Sorry, Phil." Then he'd just shrug and say, "No matter." But it did matter to him. You can imagine – with two teenage children the phone was constantly ringing, and Phil suffered a lot of hurts.

'In all the time Phil was in hospital or staying with his friends, Leslie was just one mile away. It would have been easier for him to visit than any of us. He claimed he couldn't because of all the publicity that it would cause, but there would have been no publicity if he had visited Philip at his friends' house. Or he could have worn a wig and dark glasses to get into the hospital unrecognized.'

Angela and her mother did everything they could to make Philip's last few weeks comfortable. Every Friday her mother travelled to London from Farnborough to spend the day with him. Since having a plastic hip fitted in 1978 Anne Grantham finds any travel difficult and painful, but she always managed the journey.

'Mum and Philip both loved their Fridays together. They were very happy, considering the situation. But mum was carrying a terrible burden. She wasn't allowed to talk to anyone about Philip, in case the news got out. Can anyone imagine what that did to her – not being able to tell a soul that her son was dying? After the news got out she realized that people must have thought her very callous or very ashamed not to have spoken about it – but she was neither. She and I spent hours on the phone comforting each other.'

When Philip was in hospital, they spent more hours at his bedside. So did Graham, Angela's husband.

'Graham had no problem accepting Philip for what he was. He recognized he was kind and gentle, and that was more important than whether or not he was gay. Graham is not the most tolerant person in the world, but he was able to put Philip and Philip's personality ahead of what he thought about homosexuality. Leslie obviously could not do that.'

A week before Philip died, Leslie and Jane's first baby was born. Weak as he was, Philip took a walking stick and hobbled to the shops to buy a present.

Wally, reluctant to get involved in Philip's illness until death was imminent, spent several hours with his son sorting out his will. Then Philip suggested that both Angela and his mother visit him and say their goodbyes. He wanted to spare them the agony of sitting at his bedside when the time came. Angela and Graham went to Almoth Ward, St Mary's Hospital, to see him, and the following day they drove Anne down for her turn.

'We chatted and I held his hand. He was very weak, but he remained cheerful until the very end. We talked about the time he stayed with me when he first came to work in London, and the things we'd done together as kids. Our eyes were filling with tears, but we both kept trying to be brave. He told me he was relying on me to look after mum and dad. Philip and Graham gave each other a big hug, and they were both crying. I didn't say goodbye. I just said, "God bless. I love you, Philip. I'll never forget you."

'As I was leaving he called me back and said he wanted the truth about his death to come out. You see, he wasn't ashamed of being gay, and he wasn't ashamed of having Aids. But he knew that the way Leslie had behaved, as if it was something shameful, would make it harder for other Aids victims. He had been loyal to Leslie until the end, but at the end he wanted the truth to come out.

'He had always talked about writing a book – about our childhood and the rest of his life. He wanted everyone to know what growing up in our house was like, and what living in the shadow of Leslie – first as a murderer then as a star – was like. He held my hand and said, "Do my book for me, Angela." I said, "I can't, Phil. You know I can't." But he replied, "You can, you know. You've got it all in your head. Just get it down on paper." I promised him I would try. But Philip could see the funny side of everything. He would have made his book witty and amusing. I didn't think the way Les treated him was amusing.'

When Anne left the hospital after spending two hours with Philip the following day, she was in tears. She talked about her youngest son all the way home to Farnborough, as Angela's husband Graham drove them.

The funeral was arranged by Philip's friends. Leslie did not attend; he sent flowers, with a card cunningly signed from 'L., J. and Spike' – his nickname for the baby.

The funeral cars, with the rest of the family in them, passed the end of Leslie's road on their way to the crematorium. Involuntarily, the whole family turned to look down the road at the house – a house that none of them had visited. Ironically, Philip was the only one who had ever, at that stage, been inside Leslie's home. After the funeral, the small present that Philip had bought for the baby was found by his friends. They took the neatly wrapped little parcel round to Leslie's house, but got no reply from knocking at the door. They peered through the letterbox and saw that both

Leslie and Jane were inside, so they pushed the present through the door. To this day, none of the family knows what was in the package.

Anne and Angela later collected Philip's ashes, and scattered them in the shape of a cross under a cherry tree in the grounds of the crematorium. They had hoped that Wally would make the arrangements, but he did not – and as the days went by it tore into Anne Grantham's heart that her son had not been properly laid to rest.

'She knew she would have to organize it herself, so I said I'd go with her,' says Angela. 'We went to the crematorium and put Philip's name in the book of remembrance. But we had to sort out the money side and that's when I got so cross with dad – he should have been there, at mum's side, helping her. Then we scattered the ashes.

'The funeral had been bad enough, but this was worse, especially as we were the only two there. As we were going home we had to cross a main road. Mum was so deeply upset she was like a little girl lost in a snowstorm. I had to hold her hand and tell her thatwhen I said "Go" she was to cross the road as fast as she could.'

A week after Philip died, Anne Grantham's brother John (known as Danny) from Manchester also died. He was popular with all the family, and Anne, particularly, was deeply affected. This time Leslie sent flowers openly, with his name on them. Angela was disappointed but not surprised by Leslie's behaviour.

'I believe that when death comes you should put aside personal feelings and that everybody is duty bound to ease the transition – to make dying as soft and easy as possible. If you are not capable of that, you are not a decent human being. Leslie made dying harder for Phil, because of his personal prejudices, which are founded on ignorance.'

She knew that the protection of his image was paramount to him. But her disappointment turned to anger when news of Philip's death leaked out. Leslie went into Operation Cover-up immediately. To different journalists he denied he had a brother called Philip; claimed he had not seen his brother for twenty years; denied that he knew his brother had Aids. When the story broke, the *Sun* was the only newspaper to have a photograph of Philip. A reporter went round to Leslie's house to check with him that it was a picture of his brother. By this time, with the story all over all the papers, Leslie had nothing to lose, and admitted it was Philip in the picture.

Simon and Ian, the two friends who had looked after Philip so faithfully, were besieged by reporters. They tried to avoid answering questions, but it was hard – and they owed no loyalty to Leslie Grantham. Wally and Anne and the rest of the family were also bombarded by questions from journalists. Angela pleaded with Leslie to make a statement about Philip's death, believing it would relieve the pressure on the others. He refused.

So then Angela took a decision that would tear the family in half again. She decided that if Leslie would not talk about Philip's death, she would – to the *News of the World*. She was well paid for her story, which ran in the paper for three weeks and covered the full story of how Leslie had rejected Philip, and how her parents had not been invited to Leslie's home or seen their baby grandson.

Wally, who demanded loyalty to Leslie above all else, was furious. Anne understood why Angela had done it, and even told her daughter that if she was going to do it she should feel no guilt about taking money for it – but none the less she did not condone it, certainly not in Wally's presence. John, as usual, sided with his father. Leslie was furious, and has not spoken to his sister since.

John claims that much of what Angela said, whilst

true, was twisted and bitter. He never admits directly to any chink in the armour. To John they are a devoted, happy family and there is nothing odd about the fact that he and his parents were not invited to see the new baby (at the time of writing, two years after Spike's birth, his mother, brother and sister Angela have still not seen him or his little brother). John claims that Leslie rings his parents every week, and sends them a Fortnum and Mason's hamper at Christmas.

Angela, more honest and less blindly loyal, says Leslie rings only when he needs something – usually to warn his parents and the rest of the family about some new story about to break in the newspapers, and to tell them to stay quiet.

For some time after talking to the *News of the World*, Angela was persona non grata at her parents' home in Farnborough. John, too, told the story of his mental breakdown to *Sunday*, the magazine that is free to *News of the World* readers. That, too, did not find favour with Leslie, who was upset that John had described Jane as 'posh'.

Leslie has cynically complained to showbusiness friends that he has had worse publicity that anyone except Adolf Hitler – but that some good has come from it because both his sister and his brother have paid for their houses from the proceeds of selling their stories.

Angela did make a substantial sum – certainly not the price of a new house, but enough for the deposit. But John has never made very much money from journalists – only enough to clear off his bar bill. And he lives in a run-down council flat, where the phone is cut off and the glass in the front door is smashed. He speaks of Leslie only in terms of glowing praise, and is mortified to think that anything he said upset his brother.

Angela's relationship with her parents has never

returned to normal. Her marriage to Graham broke up last year, although they parted on amicable terms. With her children seventeen and nineteen, she felt it was time to break away from a marriage that had been on the rocks for some time.

'We had had a series of family tragedies that had kept us together, but that was all that was left of the marriage. When the children were old enough, both left school and working, I realized it was time to start again. At thirty-nine I had to make my mind up while I was young enough for a fresh start,' she says.

The family home was sold up, and with her share of the proceeds Angela was able to put down the deposit on another house. She found a job as an assistant manageress in a clothes shop and, with the help of a lodger, can just afford her mortgage repayments. For a few weeks, between homes, she stayed with her parents. There was friction – every time Leslie's name was mentioned in a newspaper her father turned on her and renewed his attack for her *News of the World* series.

But Anne Grantham was covertly supportive, as she always has been to all her children. Not blindly loyal, like Wally; hers is a loyalty born of fierce pride. And friction is a way of life for the battling Granthams. Anne and Wally have a relationship just as fiery today as when they first moved with their young family to Tillingbourne Green.

Leslie has come to dominate their lives. He, and his career, are their only subject of conversation. They may be rowing about it or discussing it, but in one form or another it is on their minds all the time. They have become experts on journalism and journalists: they buy all the popular newspapers every day, scouring them for stories about Leslie. Wally, who likes to believe he is closer to his famous son than anyone else in the family, and has now even visited Leslie's home, tries to convince the others that he is Leslie's confidant. When the news about Jane having been married before was revealed, Wally claimed he had already known it. And before the second baby was born Wally told the rest of the family authoritatively that it was going to be a girl, implying that he had inside information.

He is inordinately proud that the family name is going to be perpetuated by Leslie's sons. Angela always remembers him telling her, when her children were born, that they didn't really count as grandchildren because they were not Granthams.

Her mother is still desperately hurt by the way she has been cut out of Leslie's life. He has spoken about his family in a way that is either very unfeeling, or was cold-bloodedly calculated to hurt.

'I have a love-hate relationship with my family,' he said, jokingly. 'I love them and they hate me.' Then he added, seriously, 'I don't really have anything in common with them now.' He said he had become independent during his prison years, and had 'moved on' from his family. If he hadn't he reckoned he would never have launched himself into an acting career.

On another occasion he said that his life really only began after he left prison. 'In theory, I'm still only eight years of age,' he said in 1986. 'I feel I've just been on this planet for eight years.' It was a comment that hurt his family deeply.

'Where does he think we were, all those years that he now says didn't exist?' asks Angela. 'Can you imagine how mum feels, and the rest of us, who stood by him through prison and were around all the way through his childhood? I wish we hadn't bothered visiting him and worrying about him, helping him when he came out. Because all we've had for it is the insult of being told none of it counted for anything.'

John Grantham has failed to find a full-time regular job, but works for the Manpower Services Commission whenever there is work available. He is still a charming and good-looking bloke, if somewhat of a roué. His spare time is, as ever, spent at the local pub. Since splitting up with Wendy he has been 'engaged' to marry at least two other women.

His father joins him in the pub every Sunday lunchtime, and John goes back to his parents' house for a traditional large Sunday lunch. Then the whole family watch the omnibus edition of *EastEnders*, which Wally has watched religiously during the week and videoed. He has a complete set of the soap on video. John also bought him, for a Christmas present, the BBC book about the series.

And when he goes round his ward canvassing votes for his seat on the council, Wally proudly introduces himself on the doorsteps as 'Dirty Den's dad'. He revels in the connection.

Angela, living quietly in her new home, is hoping that no new friends and neighbours will make the connection. She does not want to be known as 'Dirty Den's sister', or even as Leslie Grantham's sister. She wants nothing more than to get away from the brother she was so close to as a kid.

'Nobody who has not been in this situation can appreciate what it is like for us. We don't have our own lives. The only life that matters is Leslie's. Even the break-up of my marriage was in the papers. My kids can't even lead their own lives – they got teased at school. Whenever anyone finds out the connection, that's all they want to talk to you about. You just don't exist as a person in your own right.

'And don't expect any sympathy from Leslie. All he cares about is number one. Just like when he was a kid. Just like when he killed a man for money – money he needed.'

'Before he became famous he rang me most times when he was on the scrounge. Or if he thought that

Graham, being a policeman, could get him off his parking tickets. That's Leslie.'

Angela's greatest sadness is that, when her daughter Claire gave birth to a baby last year, the family had to hush up the birth. Not just because Claire is not married, but because the father of her baby daughter is black.

'We all know how Leslie feels about blacks. And dad's as bad,' says Angela. 'So instead of being able to make a fuss about my first grandchild, I've had to keep the whole thing quiet. It's so unfair on Claire.'

CHAPTER 13

'EastEnders' And Beyond

Within a few months of being on the air *EastEnders* was top of the audience polls. If anything justified the BBC's anxiety to produce a successful soap, that did. It countered all the popular value-for-licence-money arguments against the BBC, proving that they could compete in any sphere with their independent rivals. What's more, it achieved critical acclaim, being placed – quite rightly – on a par with its rival *Coronation Street* for good writing, acting and directing. Even the inevitable criticisms from Mary Whitehouse of strong dialogue and meaty storylines could be countered with the defence of realism.

EastEnders and *Coronation Street* are the best-quality soaps in the world, using good writers (at least two major playwrights, Jack Rosenthal and Jim Allen, cut their teeth on *Coronation Street*), consistent storylines and, for the most part, good-calibre actors. It is difficult to talk in superlatives about soap operas: with the exception of the glossy American soaps like *Dallas* and *Dynasty* they are low-budget productions working round-the-calendar, a timetable that exhausts actors, directors and writers alike. But as the critic Milton Shulman said, 'British television is the least worst in the world', so British soaps (or most of them anyway – *Crossroads* was perhaps the dishonourable exception) are the least worst in the world.

In fairness to the others, those involved in *EastEnders* and *Coronation Street* enjoy the advantage of only having to produce two shows a week. 'Only' is a strange word to use about a production schedule that has the actors rehearsing for three days and filming for three days each week, but it has to be compared to the frenetic workloads of the American daytime soaps and shows like the successful Australian *Neighbours*, which are churning out five episodes a week. At least the British shows are rehearsed – a distinction that shows.

Neighbours followed *EastEnders* into the BBC schedules, staring in October 1986 in a daytime slot but then in January 1988 being given a repeat at peak teatime viewing. With the later screening it immediately moved *en bloc* into five of the top ten ratings (averaging fifteen million viewers to *EastEnders*' twenty million). It is an inferior product in every possible way, so its success perhaps illustrates Leslie Grantham's maxim that if a cup of tea is poured often enough on the screen, the teapot will get fan mail.

Quality has, in fact, never been a prerequisite of a successful soap. The first soaps originated in America in the 1930s, when the proliferation of radio stations meant there were endless hours of air time to be filled. The need to finance the stations (unlike Britons, the Americans have never paid licence fee money for either radio or television) meant that the air time was sold in packages to sponsors, commercial firms who paid for programmes in return for plugs for their products at the beginning and end (and sometimes in the middle) of the show. As the soap manufacturing giant Procter and Gamble was one of the earliest and biggest sponsors, the long-running drama series was dubbed 'soap operas', the opera part of the name deriving probably from the level of high melodrama they achieved – something on the scale of grand opera.

The first radio soaps were moralistic in tone. They featured ordinary people at whom life threw the most appalling sequence of tragedies, yet who were able to face them stoically and blamelessly. The characters were reassuring, dependable, unchanging. The programmes were pure escapism, and their birth at the time of the Depression has given rise to the theory that soap operas only thrive when things are going badly for their audience.

Professor Laurie Taylor, the sociologist, said, 'Soap operas tend to be watched in times of economic difficulties when people are uncertain about the future. They suggest that you can solve all your problems by sitting around a table and talking about them. This can be very reassuring to people faced with real problems involving governments, nuclear missiles and worldwide stock exchange crashes.'

It is true that the Depression years and the war years marked peaks on the audience graphs of the American radio soaps. However, this theory belies the great success of *Coronation Street*, launched at the end of 1960 into a buoyant economy, when unemployment was low and society was just starting to 'swing'. It also ignores the fact that, although *EastEnders* was launched when unemployment was high, by the time *Neighbours* got its peak viewing slot the British economy had recovered substantially, unemployment was waning, and consumer spending had hit an all-time high. Although the country was allegedly divided into 'two nations', and the second, under-privileged nation of jobless may have made up a substantial part of *Neighbours'* daytime audience, there just are not enough of them to account for the massive viewing figures for the early evening slot.

No, the reason audiences love soaps is probably much simpler: people like finding out about other people. It is the basis of all gossip, which has thrived since time immemorial at work, at home, in schools – in any environment in which human beings are gathered together. Popular newspapers grow rich by sharing with their readers the ins and outs of the lives of the famous. All drama, great or small, concerns an exploration of human behaviour. The soaps are just a never-ending version of this, easy to pick up and put down at will because of the continuity of the characters.

Although they are supposed to mirror everyday life, everyday life is too boring to translate faithfully on to the screen, so the regular characters live on a diet of death, disaster, marriage, divorce, illegitimacy, pregnancy, miscarriage, theft, rape and blackmail. It is easy to poke fun at them because of this unnaturally high level of melodrama – it is even easier to become hooked on them.

Soap addiction is no respecter of intellect, class, sex or age. It may be true that more women than men are regular followers of the events in Albert Square, but the margin is close.

Britain was slow at following America into soaps, largely because of the Reithian philosophy that the BBC should lead its audience, not follow them, and also because, without the commercial strictures of American radio, the pulling power of soaps was not appreciated or valued here. The first British-produced soap was actually made during the war, but it was not for home consumption. It was called *Front Line Family*, and was beamed by the World Service at North America and Canada, as propaganda to let them know what it was like living in wartime Britain. It worked. The confusion of fiction with reality, which seems to be a major characteristic of a successful soap, brought food parcels flooding into the BBC for the mythical Robinson family in exactly the same way that money was sent in for Lofty and Michelle when they were married, and that job applications are regularly received for work as bar staff in the Queen Vic or the Rovers Return.

After the war, *Mrs Dale's Diary* was launched on

209

BBC radio, shortly followed by *The Archers*, which is Britain's longest-running soap opera at thirty-five years old (*The Guiding Light* in America has been on the air for over fifty years, starting on radio and switching to television in the fifties). The BBC's purpose in launching *The Archers* was didactic: the shortages of postwar Britain meant that farmers had to be helped to make the best possible use of their land, and it was thought that a series about farming folk would be able subliminally to encourage them to use new techniques. Although, to this day, it is faithful to its farming roots, it soon became clear that it was the romantic entanglements of the Archer clan that had an audience far wider than just farmers tuning in. In fact, when ITV was launched in 1955 it was completely upstaged, not by the opposition BBC TV, but by the radio. Sixteen million listeners tuned in to hear an episode about the death of Grace Archer.

Early television soaps were modestly successful. The best of the bunch was *Compact*. Its star, Ronnie Allen, who also starred in another BBC soap, *United*, before having a long run in *Crossroads*, believes the show was ahead of its time, and that, relaunched today, it would run away with the ratings. Set in the offices of a women's magazine, it certainly had all the right romantic ingredients. But, as *Coronation Street*, *EastEnders* and *Neighbours* all prove, the best setting for a soap is not an office but a whole community. It allows much more flexibility in terms of the age and class of the characters, as well as giving much more variety to possible storylines.

It was *Coronation Street* that first proved that a British soap could have 'legs' – the ability to run and run. Whether *EastEnders* will be in the same league cannot yet be judged, although there is no reason why it should not be. It has already survived losing some of the early characters (Angie, Lofty, punk Mary, Lou

Beale) who, initially, appeared indispensable to the viewers. Lou Beale was originally conceived as the lynchpin of the whole series, the matriarchal figure at the head of the Beale and Fowler households around whom all the action would take place. When ratings plateaued after the first few months, the strategy to boost them was to 'push Angie' – and it was because of that plan that Den, eventually to become the most powerful character of all, came so much to the fore. Yet both Anna Wing (who played Lou) and Anita Dobson (Angie) have gone.

The show wll certainly survive without Dirty Den, although it will be very difficult for the producers to create as compelling a character ever again. It is not quite like *Dallas* losing JR, which would take all the central core out of the glossy American soap. But there can be no doubt that Den will be a hard act to follow.

But *Coronation Street* survived the loss of Ena Sharples and Elsie Tanner. And, although at each loss viewers said they would thenceforth forsake their favourite soap, audience figures proved that they didn't, and a whole new generation of viewers who don't even remember the early characters have been trawled into its net.

EastEnders owes an (unacknowledged) debt to *The Street*, simply for setting high standards. Julia Smith no doubt arrived at her own belief in the necessity of good, realistic dialogue from working on shows like *Z Cars* – but they, too, had been influenced by the standard of writing on *The Street*.

However, *EastEnders* has broken new ground. It has introduced much younger characters, perhaps having learned from the success of *Grange Hill* (the nearest thing to a children's soap) that teenagers are a great source of stories and conflict, and that young actors can handle the pressure of a soap's working schedule. This, in turn, has brought a younger audience profile than

Coronation Street has. *EastEnders*, too, has pursued realism more doggedly than any other soap. Storylines are not isolated: the cot death of Sue and Ali's baby early in the series has affected the actions and words of both of those characters ever since; the rape of Kathy Beale was seen not just as the highlight for one week, but as an ongoing story in which all the after-effects of rape were explored.

Although Julia Smith and Tony Holland have made it clear that they do not include campaigning issues for the sake of campaigning, the series has covered many major social problems: unemployment, racism, sexism, homosexuality, drug-taking, prostitution, adoption, arranged marriages, Aids and alcoholism, to name but a few. It has got away from the cosiness of *Coronation Street*, where poverty is implicit rather than explicit.

Within the terms of reference of a soap opera, it has been phenomenally successful. In its second year, it picked up award after award and was given the Royal Family seal of approval when Princess Diana visited the set. Commercially, it has been a good money-spinner for the BBC. It is now sold to Canada, Australia, New Zealand, Norway, Iceland, Holland and Spain, and both Belgium and Holland can receive it on cable TV. It has made it into the top ten in both Australia and New Zealand, and it is number one on one Spanish station. In America, where it goes out in most states on PBS, it has a growing cult following. Although the BBC do not release figures for how much revenue it brings in, it was created originally for home-grown use only, so anything extra is a bonus.

Like *Coronation Street*, it has created stars out of actors and actresses who were unknowns a relatively short time ago. Some of them will prove to have a real acting ability that will transcend their soap typecasting – remember Arthur Lowe, who played Mr Swindley in

The Street but went on to become Captain Mainwaring of *Dad's Army*? He was a superb comedy actor.

Others will spend the rest of their professional lives trading on their transitory glory in Britain's top soap.

Which category will Leslie Grantham fit into?

'Are they stars – or are they only stars within the context of the programme?' asked Julia Smith, creator and executive producer of *EastEnders*.

'I'm not sure they are stars in the way an all-round actor who's played hundreds of classical roles is a star. I don't know that there's even such a thing as a soap opera star. What happens after they leave the series? They're as good as their latest soap, aren't they?'

It would be hard to convince the crowds who swarmed to meet Leslie Grantham every time he cut a ribbon to open a supermarket that he wasn't a star, but perhaps Julia Smith is right that her 'family' are only stars within the context of the programme. Once they have left the show and are no longer seen twice or more times a week in a third of all the sitting rooms in Britain, they very quickly lose their star quality.

Unless, of course, they go on to bigger and better things. After all, Ryan O'Neal and Mia Farrow both started in that corniest of corny American soaps, *Peyton Place*. Both have put that firmly behind them and gone on to superstardom. But for every O'Neal and Farrow there are a hundred more actors and actresses who have never transcended their soap origins. Will Leslie Grantham be one of those who makes the leap, or will he always be running back to Dirty Den? Perhaps the only other soap character to have had the same impact in Britain was Pat Phoenix, who played Elsie Tanner in *Coronation Street* – and she never managed to put Elsie behind her, despite her abilities as an actress.

Whatever they think of him personally, those who

have worked with Leslie closely on *EastEnders* respect him as an actor. He has been unfailingly punctual, always knows his lines, never misses rehearsals, doesn't upstage others and completes his scenes with a minimum of fuss. But those are qualities of professionalism, not stardom. His screen presence has proved at times to be electrifying – he has certainly got the sex appeal that Julia Smith suspected at his audition, and the capacity to make those watching him 'sit up by his sheer presence', as did Simon Dunmore, who gave him his job in rep at Coventry. But although he has been scathing about his fellow actors, describing them as 'from the MFI school of acting – wooden', his own performance has often been lacklustre. Ironically, the prison scenes – in which he of all people *should* have been convincing – have been the worst of the whole series, probably because the writing has not been as good, the characters he has had around him have been cardboard cutouts, and he himself has seemed edgy and uneasy.

Allan O'Keefe, a very experienced actor who played the father of punk girl Mary in the series, and who lectures on television, believes that Leslie Grantham is capable of far greater acting than he has been called upon to produce for *EastEnders*.

'The trouble for Les is that the part of Den comes too easy. He's one of the best actors in the show, but he's playing a version of himself so it isn't stretching him. He needs to do other work, worry about it a bit, and he'll prove he's a good-class actor. He should have left *EastEnders* a long time ago. He's been wasting his talent. Not because working in a soap isn't as demanding an acting job as you'll get, but because he's not getting enough variety.'

Others, who prefer not to be named, believe that Leslie has been playing the only part he is capable of playing: himself. And that unless he chooses roles that similarly dovetail with his own background, accent and personality, he will fail. But there are stars who have achieved fame and fortune doing just that (Michael Caine, however diverse the roles he plays, invests them all with the unmistakable stamp of his own personality), and no one who knows him suspects that Leslie harbours any deep ambition to join the Royal Shakespeare Company.

What motivates Leslie Grantham now, just as it has all his life, is money. Success to him is a vehicle to make himself rich, and his prime concern is to capitalize on his fame as much as he can. He said at the height of the *EastEnders* mania, before his second son was born:

'They could kill me off. No one is indispensable to the show. So I shall try to make enough money so that my future is secure. If anything happens to me, Jane and the baby are looked after.'

Although he claims to have little in common with Dirty Den, he might recognize something of himself in Den's philosophy, as expounded in one of the early programmes:

'What's it they say? If you can't get what you want, want what you can get. Well, I've tried that. It doesn't work. I'm going to get everything I want all right. And that's the difference between me and the people around here. They want what they can get.'

It was for wanting more that he put himself through the grind of endless lucrative personal appearances, which he obviously did not enjoy (on one occasion he blushed and stammered on stage at a nightclub when a raucous crowd of women shouted obscene questions to him, and at other less harrowing appearances he still looked distinctly uncomfortable).

That is why he told a journalist that it was not just out of finer feelings for the widow of the man he had shot that he had turned down offers of £100,000 and more from newspapers to tell the full story of the murder case. He said he wasn't just being 'Mr Nice

215

Guy', but was also saving the story in order to write his own book, a book he knows would be worth a small fortune.

It is his over-riding self-interest that has gradually alienated many of his fellow-actors in *EastEnders*.

'He's always put himself first in everything,' says one of the cast. 'He'll be funny and friendly and will even do favours for people as long as it suits him to, but the minute he really wants something for himself, he changes. We hardly exist.

'He makes friends at a superficial level, especially with men. He's a man's man, he can crack jokes with the best of them. But the friendships never go deep, there's no one he's really close to. He likes to hobnob with anyone important, like Julia Smith, and he'll turn on a lot of charm with someone like her.

'He seems to get bored with people very easily. You see him glaze over and retreat inside himself.'

Leslie has countered the criticism that he is sometimes distant and silent with other members of the cast by saying that he is simply trying to memorize his lines. But they don't accept that.

Ironically, it was when he suspected Julia Smith of using him (and his past conviction) as cynically and as coldly as he uses other people that his relationship with her foundered. He came to believe that she exploited his jail history to promote *EastEnders* from the very beginning – which, if he is honest, is probably what he would have done in her shoes.

Quite how cold and hard he is is best exemplified in his dealings with his own family. His sister Angela, who grew up closest to him, no longer has any contact with him. Yet, if he is honest, he would admit that had one of his siblings been the famous member of the family, he might well have been happy to sell his story if the money had been right. And for Angela the prime motivation was not money. It was to put the record straight for her dead brother, the gentle, gay Philip who died the lingering and anguished death of an Aids victim.

'Leslie's weird, unusual,' says Angela. 'He has always taken the quickest way to everything. He's a worker, but if he can see a way of cutting corners, he will. He has done it since he was small. His own needs are more important than anyone else's. He's totally self-centred. He'll always pass the buck – he hasn't got a lot of conscience. When he was a child I saw him take the cane for things he didn't do – but only if it suited him. Another time he'd just smile when someone else took the rap for something he'd done. There's always a reason for everything Leslie does. He doesn't do anything without working out what's in it for him.

'He's got a very unusual slant on life. He thinks he got a raw deal in our childhood, but he didn't. Life was more rough and tumble then, there was always lots of argy-bargy in our house, and sometimes he would be on the receiving end of it. But mostly he and John got away with everything.

'He was the only one in the family who could have committed a murder. Mum and I would not have believed it if it had been Philip or John – but Leslie, yes. He had the coldness in him to do that. He had the strongest personality – I'm more like him than the others, but my heart is kinder than his. The way he has behaved since prison is the same as he behaved as a child, only more so. Prison didn't change him. It took what was already there and enhanced it, made him even harder. He feels he lost a lot of his life, and he will make the rest work no matter what.

'I don't know where he got his love of money, although dad, too, is strongly motivated by material things. Mum, who came from a background where there was more money, has never been impressed by it. She can rub along without it. So can I, so can John.

Philip could have done, too, but he never really had to. He worked hard to make sure he was always comfortable. But Leslie as a child was dominated by money and the things that money can bring you. It was more important to him than anything else.'

Angela feels that Leslie's success will be limited.

'I believe money was his downfall once and it will be his downfall again. One day that greed will backfire on him, like it did before. He didn't learn any lessons going to prison – not lessons about what's important in life. Otherwise he would never have treated our family as shabbily as he has done.

'He's too clever to actually never keep in touch with mum and dad, because if he did that people would be able to criticize him. No – he makes the minimum amount of contact, just the odd phone call every so often, so that no one can quite say he has cut them off.'

Angela also believes that Leslie is heading for trouble by trying to ignore his own past, and getting so upset when newspapers write about it. 'If you acknowledge his acting, you've got to acknowledge his crime. He likes to behave as though it was a different person who committed that murder. But that means he's bottling it up, not facing up to it. He never talks about it now, although before *EastEnders* he used to mention prison a lot. He has never once apologized to his family for all the trouble it brought us, nor has he ever thanked us for standing by him through those years. You don't do things in order to get thanked, but it hurts when you are not acknowledged at all.'

Angela believes that eventually Leslie will go to live in Australia, near Jane's family. 'If he could get into the family business, I'm sure he would be happy. I believe he won't mind giving up acting as long as he can find something else that brings the money in.'

She believes he could have used his position as a celebrity to do a lot of good. 'He could have done a lot for Aids victims by simply speaking up about Phil, not acting as though he was ashamed of him. And he could do more for youngsters who get into trouble with the law, like he did.'

And she shares with his mother Anne the belief that he should have made some reparation to the Reese family. 'Mum and I both think he should have paid some money to the widow. We know that money can't compensate for her loss, but at least it would be a gesture – it would show he had not forgotten what he did to them.'

Another shrewd Grantham observer, T. Dan Smith, who spent time in Ley Hill Prison with him, also believes that Leslie is laying up trouble for himself by not acknowledging his past. Since coming out of prison Dan has worked for charitable organizations helping ex-prisoners and youngsters who are running up against the law. He has appealed to Leslie to help, even if only by lending his name to the work, but without success.

'Les could get through to such a big audience – do such a lot of good. I believe that by pretending his past doesn't exist he is not only harming those he could have helped, but he is damaging himself.

'He is who he is now – a successful actor – because he was in prison. I doubt he would have done it otherwise. So he owes a debt to those who are still there. Somebody gave him some opportunities – he should now be opening them up for others.

'Like other ex-prisoners I know who have become successful, he is not conscious that any of his development is due to having been inside. Their recollections of themselves are entirely fictional. He talks about only being as old as the number of years since he left prison. That's nonsense. We are all formed by all our experiences, good or bad.

'He's the only life prisoner who is now idolized. It's a rare and obviously sometimes difficult position. People

219

will shoot him down, mentally. I believe he should face up to his own past, get involved with charitable work concerning ex-prisoners, and also get involved in public debate about prisons, juvenile delinquents and the like. That kind of intellectual ability is latent in him, but he hasn't developed it. It would provide him with the ability to face up to what he did and cope with how it has affected him. It would arm him so that one day he could discuss his crime with his children and grandchildren, because he has to face the fact that they will find out about it. He can't bury his head in the sand about it, not when he's in such a prominent position.

'There must be dark corners of his life when he thinks about what he did. He can't always shut it out. But he could shed light in there by facing up to it – and in so doing help others. That would give him a feeling of at least atoning in part for his crime.'

If he does not, Dan believes Leslie's mental stability will be at stake. He felt that Leslie was sufficiently close to being unbalanced while he was in prison to wonder whether a career in drama was a good idea. 'I felt he wasn't stable enough to cope with the ups and downs of that profession, but he has proved me wrong so far.'

While he was in prison with Leslie, Dan wrote a poem entitled 'The Lifer', based on his composite impressions of Leslie Grantham and other prisoners who were serving life sentences. The opening lines go:

> *Don't always think of me as a brutish*
> *Violent man,*
> *Although sometimes I am,*
> *But rather think of me as you*
> *Who, in one brief moment*
> *Unpremeditated, committed*
>
> *An act at once regretted.*

If those lines seem apposite to the story of Leslie Grantham's life, how much more apposite are the final lines, with the prophecy they contain for the rest of his life:

> *My sentence without end*
> *Begins.*
> *Nor will it ever end.*
> *Even when I am given*
> *Release,*
> *How can I ever know*
> *Peace?*